HarperCollins World History Atlas

S0-AAC-191

Contents

HarperCollins *CollegePublishers*

Copyright © 1996 Magellan Geographix, Inc, 6464 Hollister Avenue, Santa Barbara, CA 93117, (800) 929-4MAP.

HarperCollins® and ® are registered trademarks of HarperCollins Publishers Inc.
All rights reserved. Printed in the United States of America. No part of this book may be used or reproduced in any manner whatsoever without written permission. For information, address HarperCollins College Publishers, 10 East 53rd Street, New York, NY 10022.   *For information about any HarperCollins title, product, or resource, please visit our World Wide Web site at*   ***http://www.harpercollins.com/college*** .
Cover Image: Map of Asia by Antonio Varese. Palazzo Farnese, Caprarola, Italy. Courtesy Giraudon/Art Resource, NY.
Executive Editor: Bruce Borland. Supplements Editor: Jessica Bayne. Cover Design: Paul Lacy. Production: Rohnda Barnes.

ISBN: 0-673-98177-0

96 97 98 99 9 8 7 6 5 4 3 2

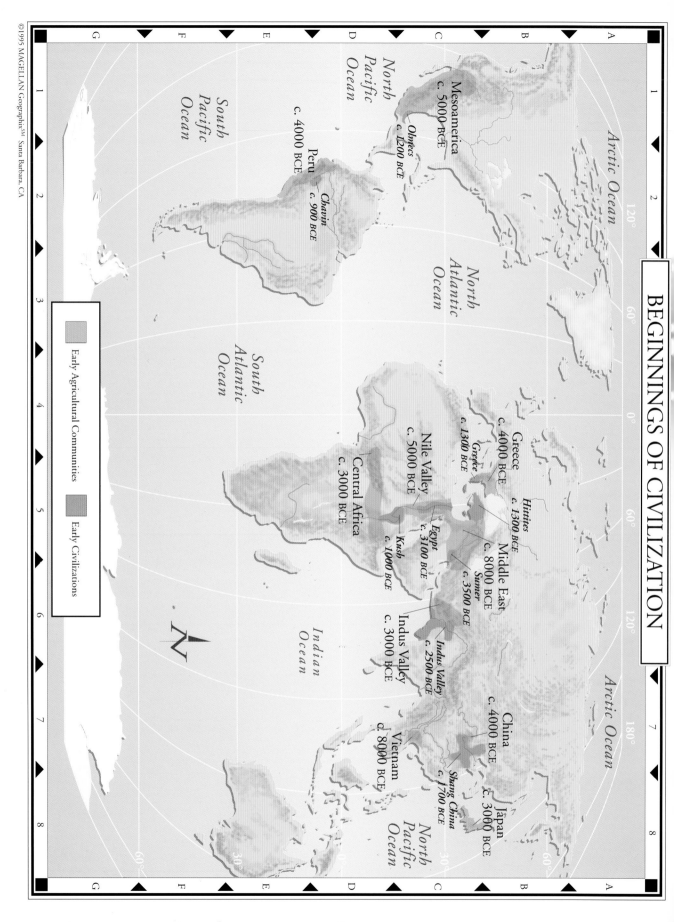

BEGINNINGS OF CIVILIZATION

Early Agricultural Communities

Early Civilizations

Mesoamerica
c. 5000 BCE

Olmec
c. 1200 BCE

Peru
c. 4000 BCE

Chavin
c. 900 BCE

Greece
c. 4000 BCE

Greece
c. 1300 BCE

Hittites
c. 1300 BCE

Middle East
c. 8000 BCE

Sumer
c. 3500 BCE

Nile Valley
c. 5000 BCE

Egypt
c. 3100 BCE

Central Africa
c. 3000 BCE

Kush
c. 1000 BCE

Indus Valley
c. 3000 BCE

Indus Valley
c. 2500 BCE

China
c. 4000 BCE

Japan
c. 3000 BCE

Shang China
c. 1700 BCE

Vietnam
c. 8000 BCE

Arctic Ocean

North Pacific Ocean

North Atlantic Ocean

South Pacific Ocean

South Atlantic Ocean

Indian Ocean

North Pacific Ocean

Arctic Ocean

N

©1995 MAGELLAN Geographix℠ Santa Barbara, CA

2

THE ANCIENT NEAR EAST

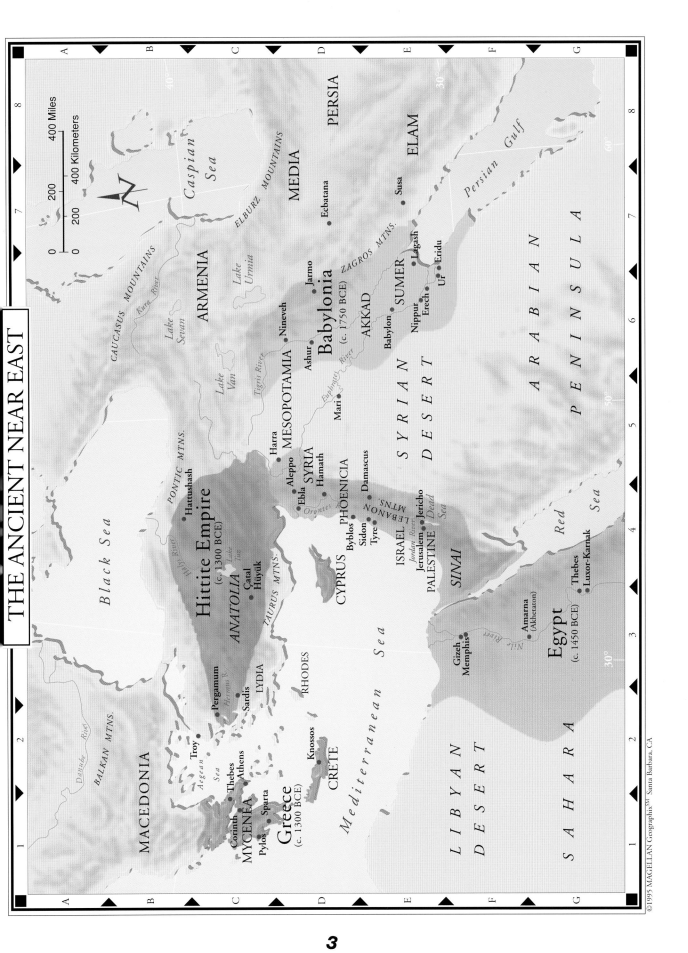

MACEDONIA

Black Sea

BALKAN MTNS.

Danube River

Troy

Thebes
Athens
Corinth
MYCENAE
Pylos
Sparta

Greece
(c. 1300 BCE)

Aegean
Sea

Knossos

CRETE

Mediterranean Sea

RHODES

LYDIA
Sardis
Pergamum

Hermus R.

Halys River

PONTIC MTNS.

Hattushash

Hittite Empire
(c. 1300 BCE)

ANATOLIA

Çatal
Hüyük

Lake
Tuz

TAURUS MTNS.

CYPRUS

Byblos
Sidon
Tyre

PHOENICIA

Aleppo
Ebla

Orontes

SYRIA
Hamath

Damascus

LEBANON MTNS.

ISRAEL
Jericho
Jerusalem
PALESTINE

Jordan River

Dead
Sea

SINAI

Red Sea

Gizeh
Memphis

Nile River

Amarna
(Akhetaton)

Egypt
(c. 1450 BCE)

Thebes
Luxor-Karnak

LIBYAN DESERT

SAHARA

30°

Harra

MESOPOTAMIA

Mari

Euphrates River

Tigris River

Lake
Van

Ashur

Nineveh

Jarmo

Babylonia
(c. 1750 BCE)

AKKAD

Babylon

SUMER

Nippur
Erech
Lagash
Ur
Eridu

SYRIAN DESERT

ARABIAN PENINSULA

50°

ARMENIA

Lake
Sevan

Lake
Urmia

Kura River

CAUCASUS MOUNTAINS

Caspian
Sea

ELBURZ MOUNTAINS

40°

MEDIA

Echatana

ZAGROS MTNS.

Susa

ELAM

PERSIA

Persian Gulf

30°

60°

400 Miles
400 Kilometers

0   200   400

N

EARLY CIVILIZATION IN ASIA

Legend:
- Shang 1500-1100 BCE
- Western Zhou 1100-1000 BCE
- Indus Valley civilization 3000-1000 BCE

N

Scale:
- 0 — 500 — 1000 Miles
- 0 — 500 — 1000 Kilometers

Labels on map:

Caspian Sea

Euphrates River

Tigris River

ZAGROS MOUNTAINS

Persian Gulf

PLATEAU OF IRAN

BACTRIA

Route of the Aryan Invasion

BALUCHISTAN

Mohenjo Daro

Arabian Sea

Indus River

HINDU KUSH MTNS.

THAR DESERT

Harappa

Kalibangan

Jhelum River

DECCAN PLATEAU

Godavari River

Krishna R.

Narmada River

HIMALAYAS

Ganges River

PLATEAU OF TIBET

Brahmaputra River

Cochin

Madurai

CEYLON

Indian Ocean

Bay of Bengal

Irrawaddy River

Salween River

Mekong River

GOBI DESERT

ORDOS DESERT

Huang River

Wei River

WESTERN ZHOU

Xi'an

Luoyang

Zhengzhou

Chang River

Huai River

SHANG

Anyang

Hemudu

Yellow Sea

Pacific Ocean

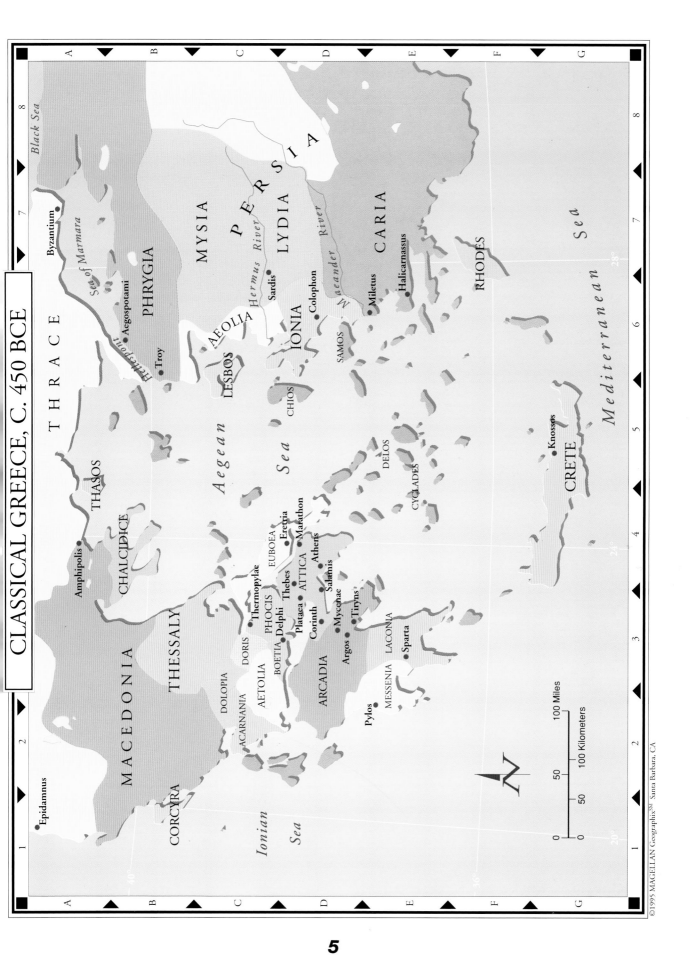

CLASSICAL GREECE, C. 450 BCE

©1995 MAGELLAN Geographix℠ Santa Barbara, CA

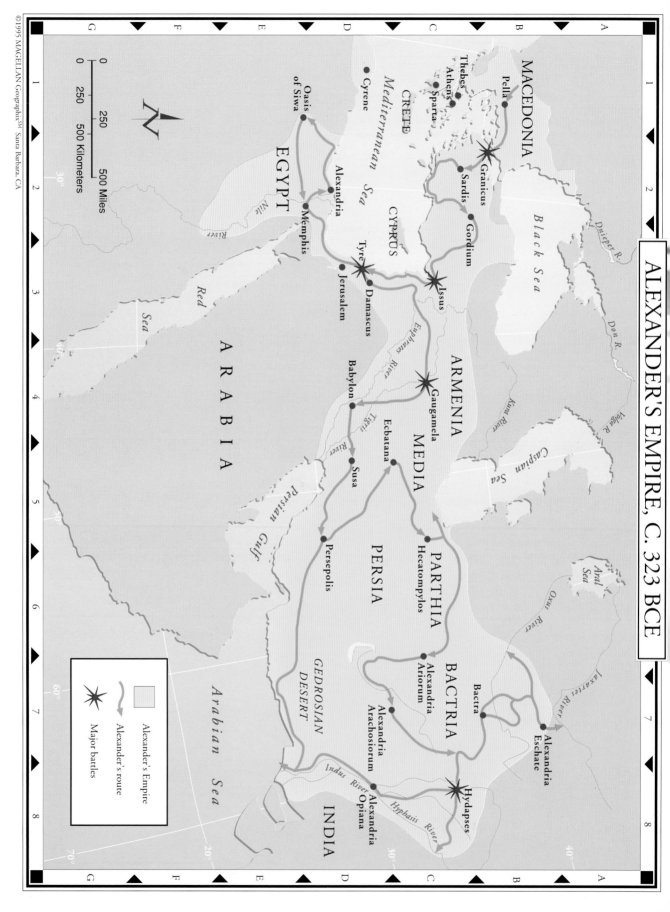

ALEXANDER'S EMPIRE, C. 323 BCE

Legend:
- Alexander's Empire
- Alexander's route
- Major battles

Scale:
0 250 500 Miles
0 250 500 Kilometers

N

Places and features labeled on map:

MACEDONIA, Pella, Granicus, Thebes, Athens, Sparta, Cyrene, CRETE, Mediterranean Sea, Sardis, Gordium, CYPRUS, Tyre, Issus, Damascus, Jerusalem, Alexandria, Memphis, Oasis of Siwa, EGYPT, Nile River, Red Sea, ARABIA, Black Sea, Dnieper R., Don R., ARMENIA, Euphrates River, Tigris River, Gaugamela, Babylon, Ecbatana, Susa, MEDIA, Caspian Sea, Volga R., Kura River, Aral Sea, Oxus River, Jaxartes River, PARTHIA, Hecatompylos, PERSIA, Persepolis, Persian Gulf, Arabian Sea, GEDROSIAN DESERT, BACTRIA, Bactra, Alexandria Ariorum, Alexandria Arachosiorum, Alexandria Eschate, Alexandria Opiana, Hydaspes, Hyphasis River, Indus River, INDIA

ANCIENT ASIA

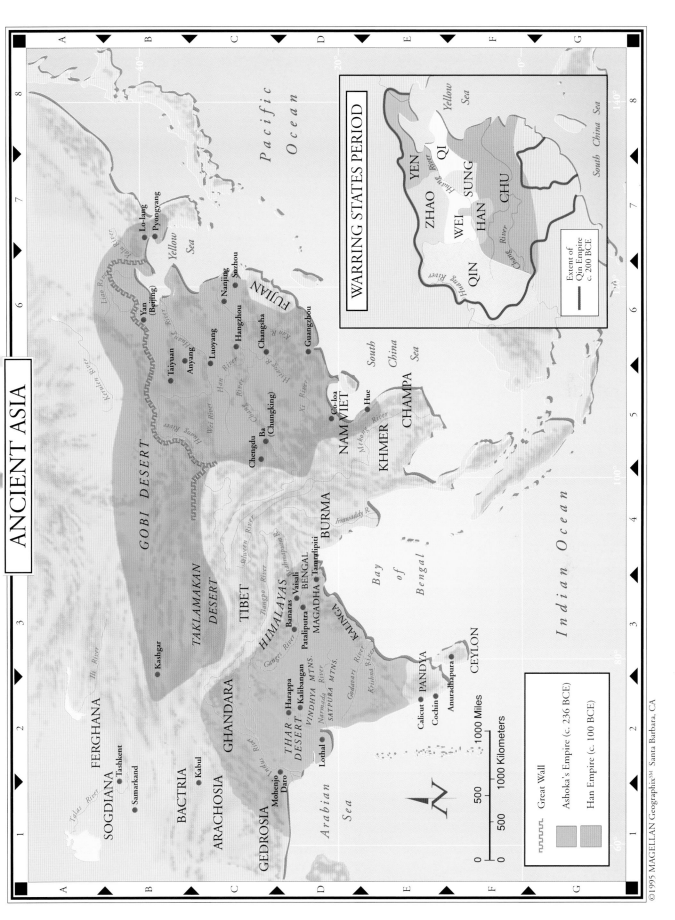

WARRING STATES PERIOD

YEN
ZHAO
QI
WEI
HAN
SUNG
QIN
CHU

Yellow Sea

South China Sea

Huang River
Chang River

Extent of
Qin Empire
c. 200 BCE

SOGDIANA
FERGHANA
Tashkent
Samarkand
BACTRIA
Kabul
ARACHOSIA
GHANDARA
GEDROSIA
Mohenjo Daro
THAR DESERT
Lothal
Harappa
Kalibangan
VINDHYA MTNS.
SATPURA MTNS.
Banaras
Pataliputra
MAGADHA
BENGAL
Vaisali
Tamralipiti
KALINGA
PANDYA
Calicut
Cochin
Anuradhapura
CEYLON

Kashgar
TAKLAMAKAN DESERT
GOBI DESERT
TIBET
HIMALAYAS
BURMA
Irrawaddy R.
Bay of Bengal

Taiyuan
Anyang
Luoyang
Nanjing
Suzhou
Hangzhou
Changsha
Guangzhou
FUJIAN
Chengdu
Ba (Chungking)
Co-loa
NAM VIET
Hue
CHAMPA
KHMER

Lo-lang
Pyongyang
Yan (Beijing)
Yellow Sea

Pacific Ocean

South China Sea

Indian Ocean

Arabian Sea

Talas River
Ili River
Liao River
Yalu River
Kerulen River
Huang River
Wei River
Han River
Chang River
Hsing R.
Xi River
Kan R.
Salween River
Mekong River
Brahmaputra R.
Ganges River
Godavari River
Krishna River
Narmada River
Indus River
Yangtze River

N

0   500   1000 Miles
0   500   1000 Kilometers

Great Wall
Ashoka's Empire (c. 236 BCE)
Han Empire (c. 100 BCE)

©1995 MAGELLAN Geographix℠ Santa Barbara, CA

7

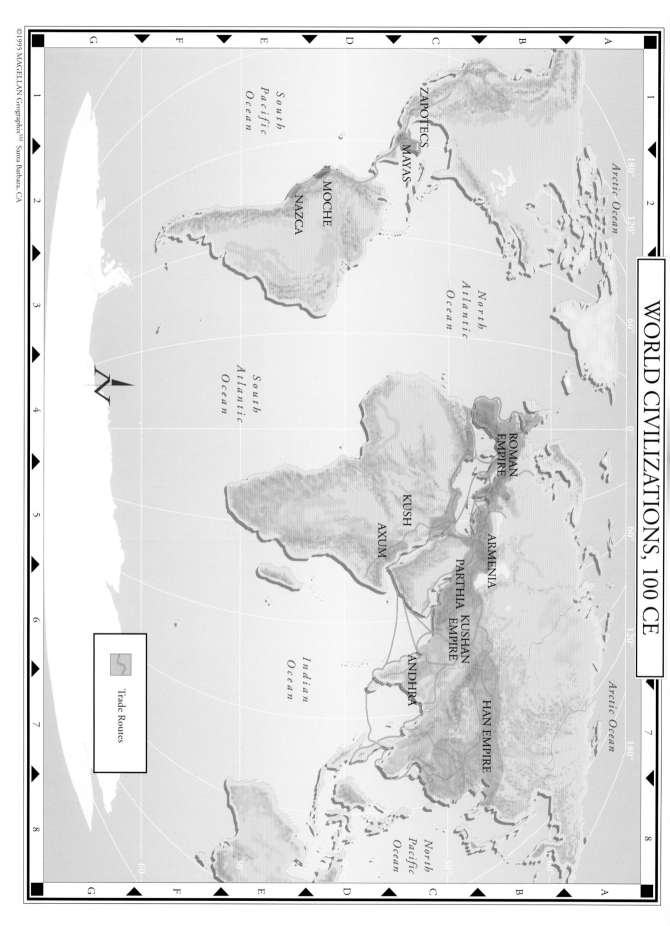

WORLD CIVILIZATIONS, 100 CE

Trade Routes

ZAPOTECS
MAYAS
MOCHE
NAZCA

ROMAN EMPIRE
ARMENIA
PARTHIA
KUSHAN EMPIRE
KUSH
AXUM
ANDHRA
HAN EMPIRE

Arctic Ocean
South Pacific Ocean
North Atlantic Ocean
South Atlantic Ocean
Indian Ocean
North Pacific Ocean

GROWTH OF THE ROMAN EMPIRE, 44 BCE TO 117 CE

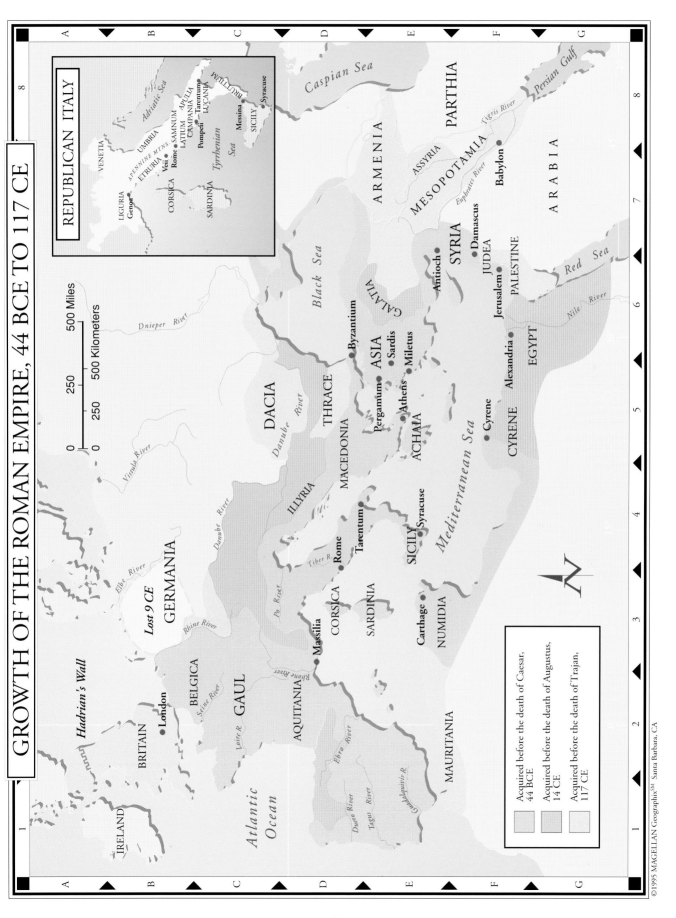

REPUBLICAN ITALY

Legend:
- Acquired before the death of Caesar, 44 BCE
- Acquired before the death of Augustus, 14 CE
- Acquired before the death of Trajan, 117 CE

Scale:
- 500 Miles
- 0 250 500 Kilometers

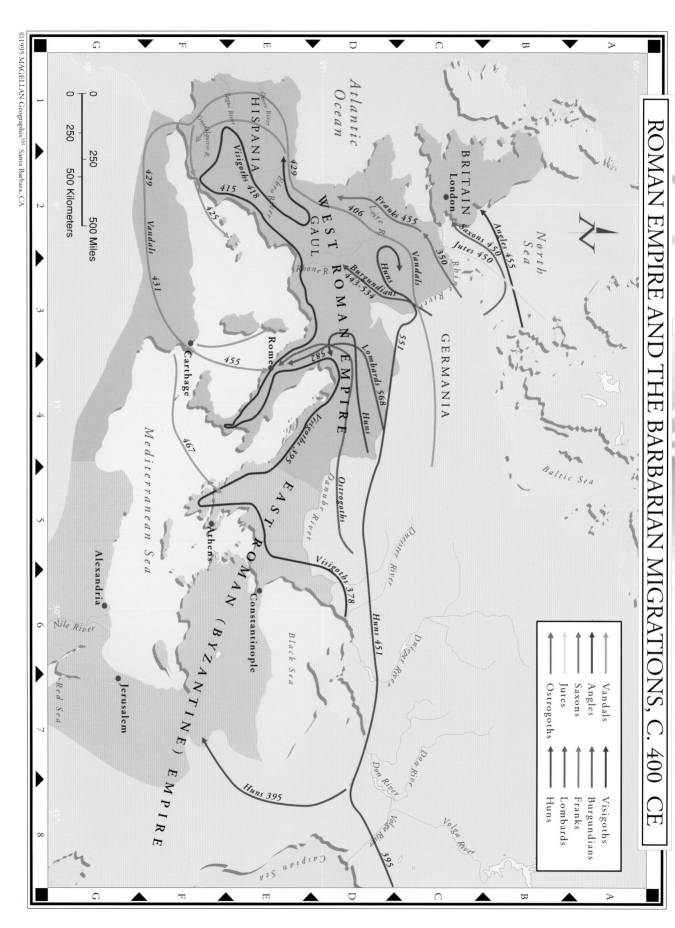

ROMAN EMPIRE AND THE BARBARIAN MIGRATIONS, C. 400 CE

©1995 MAGELLAN Geographix℠ Santa Barbara, CA

Legend:
- Vandals
- Angles
- Saxons
- Jutes
- Ostrogoths
- Visigoths
- Burgundians
- Franks
- Lombards
- Huns

EUROPE AND THE BYZANTINE EMPIRE, C. 526 CE

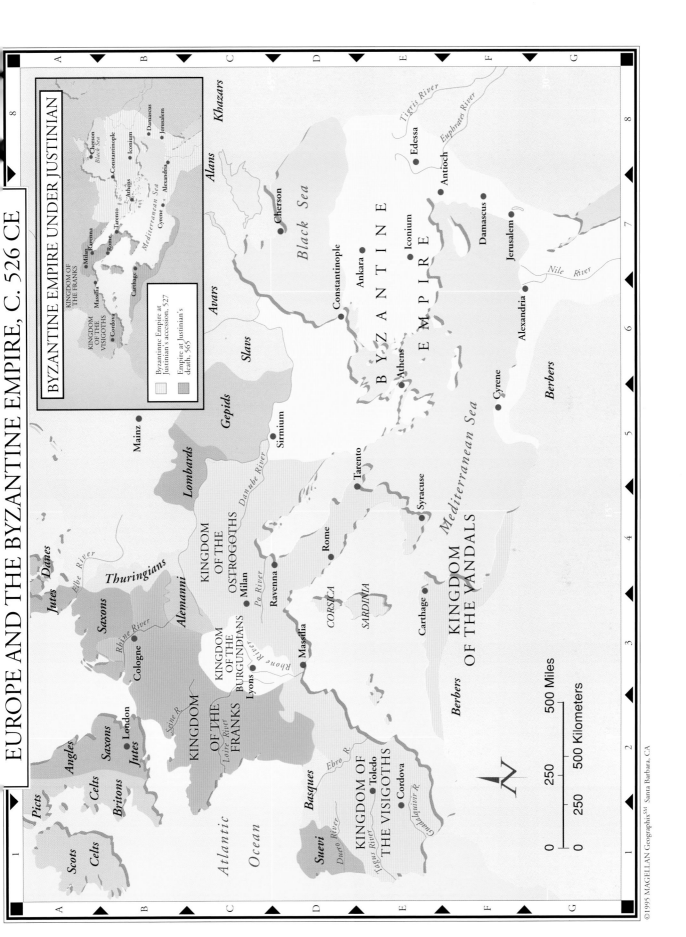

BYZANTINE EMPIRE UNDER JUSTINIAN

KINGDOM OF THE FRANKS

KINGDOM OF THE VISIGOTHS

Cherson · Black Sea · Constantinople · Iconium · Damascus · Jerusalem

Milan · Ravenna · Rome · Tarento · Athens · Mediterranean Sea · Cyrene · Alexandria

Massilia · Cordova · Carthage

Byzantine Empire at Justinian's accession, 527

Empire at Justinian's death, 565

Khazars

Alans

Avars

Slavs

Gepids

Lombards

Mainz

Thuringians

Danes

Jutes

Saxons

Alemanni

Cologne · Rhine River

KINGDOM OF THE OSTROGOTHS

Milan

Ravenna · Po River

Sirmium · Danube River

Tarento

Syracuse

Rome

CORSICA

SARDINIA

Carthage

KINGDOM OF THE VANDALS

Berbers

Massilia

KINGDOM OF THE BURGUNDIANS

Lyons · Rhône River · Loire River · Seine R.

KINGDOM OF THE FRANKS

London

Angles · Saxons · Jutes

Picts · Celts · Britons · Scots · Celts

Atlantic Ocean

Basques

Suevi · Duero River · Tagus River · Guadalquivir R. · Ebro River

KINGDOM OF THE VISIGOTHS

Toledo · Cordova

Berbers

Mediterranean Sea

BYZANTINE EMPIRE

Constantinople

Ankara

Athens

Iconium

Cherson

Black Sea

Edessa · Tigris River · Euphrates River

Antioch

Damascus

Jerusalem

Alexandria · Nile River

Cyrene

Berbers

N

500 Miles

0   250   500 Kilometers

0   250   500

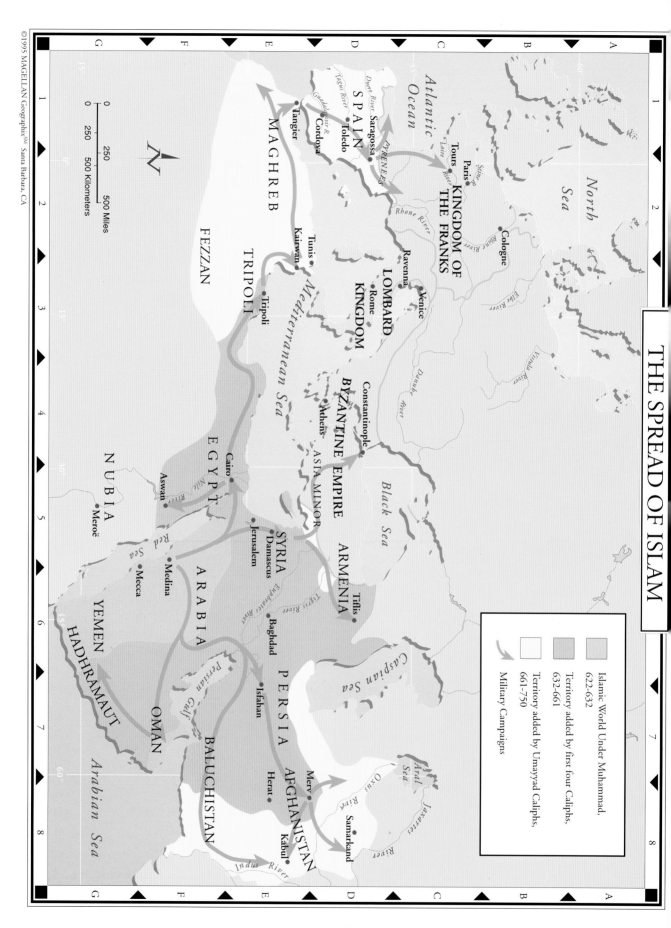

Islamic World Under Muhammad,
622-632

Territory added by first four Caliphs,
632-661

Territory added by Umayyad Caliphs,
661-750

Military Campaigns

North
Sea

Atlantic
Ocean

KINGDOM OF
THE FRANKS

Paris
Tours
Cologne
Ravenna
Venice

LOMBARD
KINGDOM
Rome

SPAIN
Saragossa
Toledo
Cordova
Tangier

MAGHREB

FEZZAN

TRIPOLI
Tripoli

Tunis
Kairwan

Mediterranean Sea

BYZANTINE
EMPIRE
Constantinople
Athens
ASIA MINOR

Black Sea

ARMENIA
Tiflis

Caspian Sea

Elbe River
Rhine River
Danube River
Vistula River
Oder River
Rhone River
Seine R.
Loire River

Duero River
Tagus River
Guadalquivir R.

PYRENEES

EGYPT
Cairo
Aswan

NUBIA
Meroë

Nile River

Red Sea

ARABIA
Medina
Mecca

YEMEN

HADHRAMAUT

OMAN

Arabian Sea

SYRIA
Damascus
Jerusalem

Baghdad

Euphrates River
Tigris River

PERSIA
Isfahan

Persian Gulf

BALUCHISTAN

AFGHANISTAN
Kabul
Herat
Merv
Samarkand

Oxus River
Jaxartes River
Aral Sea

Indus River

N

0   250   500 Miles
0   250   500 Kilometers

12

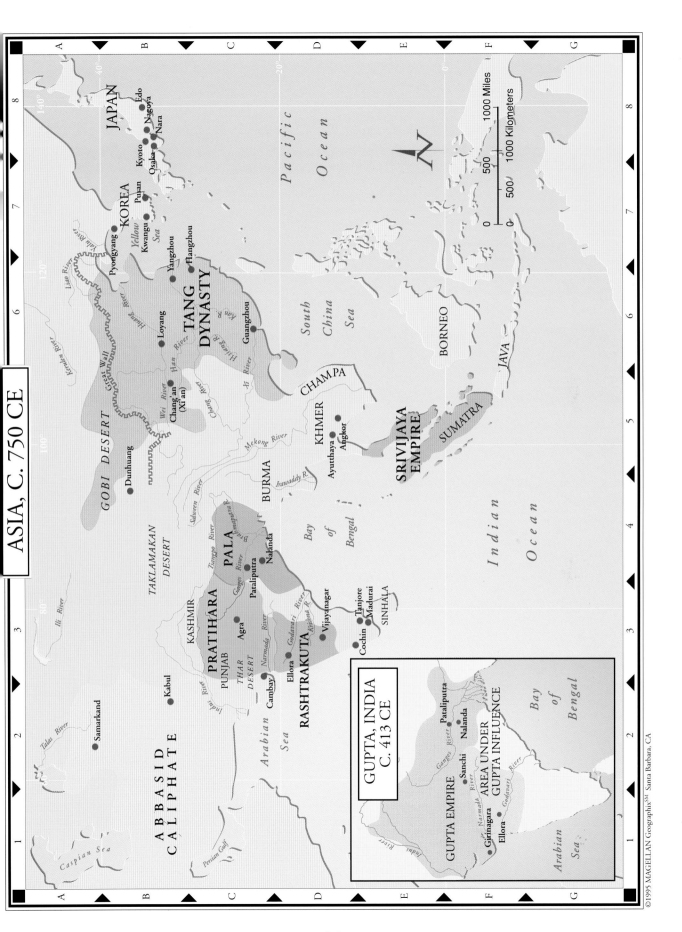

ASIA, C. 750 CE

ABBASID CALIPHATE

Samarkand

Kabul

KASHMIR

PRATIHARA

PUNJAB

Agra

THAR DESERT

Cambay

Ellora

RASHTRAKUTA

Vijayanagar

Tanjore
Madurai
Cochin

SINHALA

PALA

Pataliputra
Nalanda

Narmada River
Godavari River
Krishna R.

Arabian Sea

Persian Gulf

Caspian Sea

Talas River

Ili River

Indus River

Kerulen River

Liao River

Yalu River

GOBI DESERT

TAKLAMAKAN DESERT

Dunhuang

Great Wall

TANG DYNASTY

Chang'an (Xi'an)
Loyang
Yangzhou
Hangzhou
Guangzhou

Wei River
Huang River
Han River
Chung River
Ya River
Hsi River R
Kan R.

KOREA

Pyongyang
Kwangu
Pusan

Yellow Sea

JAPAN

Edo
Nagoya
Nara
Kyoto
Osaka

Pacific Ocean

South China Sea

BURMA

Irrawaddy R.
Salween River
Mekong River
Brahmaputra R.
Tsangpo River
Ganges River

Bay of Bengal

CHAMPA

KHMER

Ayuthaya
Angkor

SRIVIJAYA EMPIRE

SUMATRA

BORNEO

JAVA

Indian Ocean

N

1000 Miles
500
0

1000 Kilometers
500
0

GUPTA, INDIA C. 413 CE

GUPTA EMPIRE

Pataliputra
Nalanda
Sanchi
Girinagara
Ellora

AREA UNDER GUPTA INFLUENCE

Ganges River
Narmada River
Godavari River
Indus River

Bay of Bengal

Arabian Sea

THE CAROLINGIAN EMPIRE

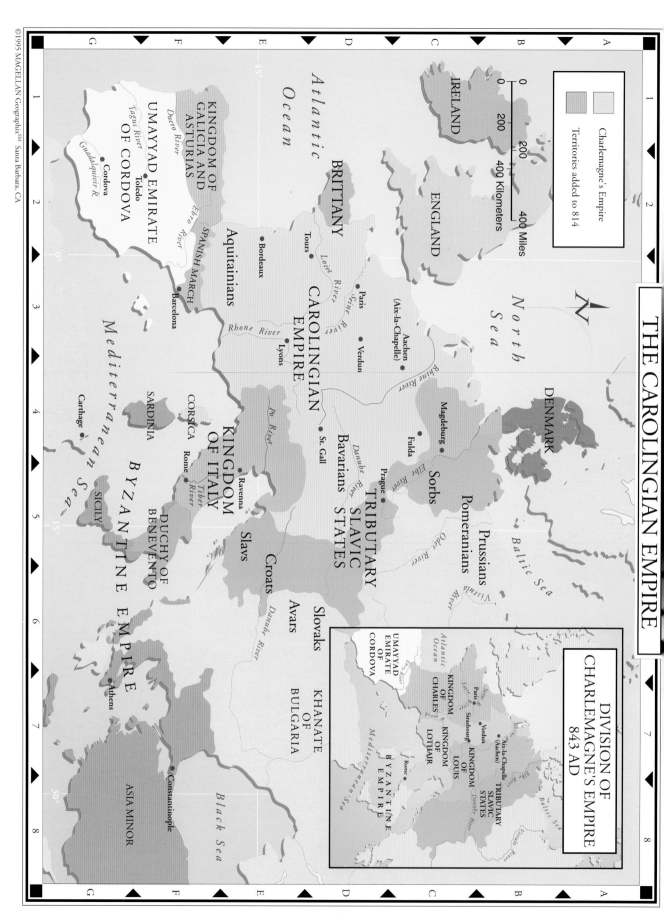

Charlemagne's Empire

Territories added to 814

DIVISION OF CHARLEMAGNE'S EMPIRE 843 AD

IRELAND

ENGLAND

BRITTANY

Atlantic Ocean

North Sea

Baltic Sea

DENMARK

Pomeranians

Prussians

Sorbs

TRIBUTARY SLAVIC STATES

Bavarians

Slavs

Croats

Avars

Slovaks

KHANATE OF BULGARIA

CAROLINGIAN EMPIRE

Aachen (Aix-la-Chapelle)

Paris

Verdun

Lyons

Tours

Bordeaux

Aquitainians

KINGDOM OF GALICIA AND ASTURIAS

UMAYYAD EMIRATE OF CORDOVA

Cordova

Toledo

Barcelona

SPANISH MARCH

Tagus River

Guadalquivir R.

Duero River

Ebro River

Rhone River

Loire River

Seine River

Rhine River

Elbe River

Oder River

Vistula River

Danube River

Po River

Tiber River

Magdeburg

Fulda

Prague

St. Gall

Ravenna

Rome

KINGDOM OF ITALY

DUCHY OF BENEVENTO

SARDINIA

CORSICA

Carthage

SICILY

Mediterranean Sea

BYZANTINE EMPIRE

Athens

Constantinople

Black Sea

ASIA MINOR

Danube River

N

0

200

400 Kilometers

0

200

400 Miles

45°

0°

15°

30°

DIVISION OF CHARLEMAGNE'S EMPIRE 843 AD

UMAYYAD EMIRATE OF CORDOVA

Atlantic Ocean

KINGDOM OF CHARLES

Paris

Strasbourg

Verdun

Aix-la-Chapelle (Aachen)

KINGDOM OF LOUIS

KINGDOM OF LOTHAR

TRIBUTARY SLAVIC STATES

Rome

BYZANTINE EMPIRE

Mediterranean Sea

Baltic Sea

Elbe River

Danube River

Vistula River

14

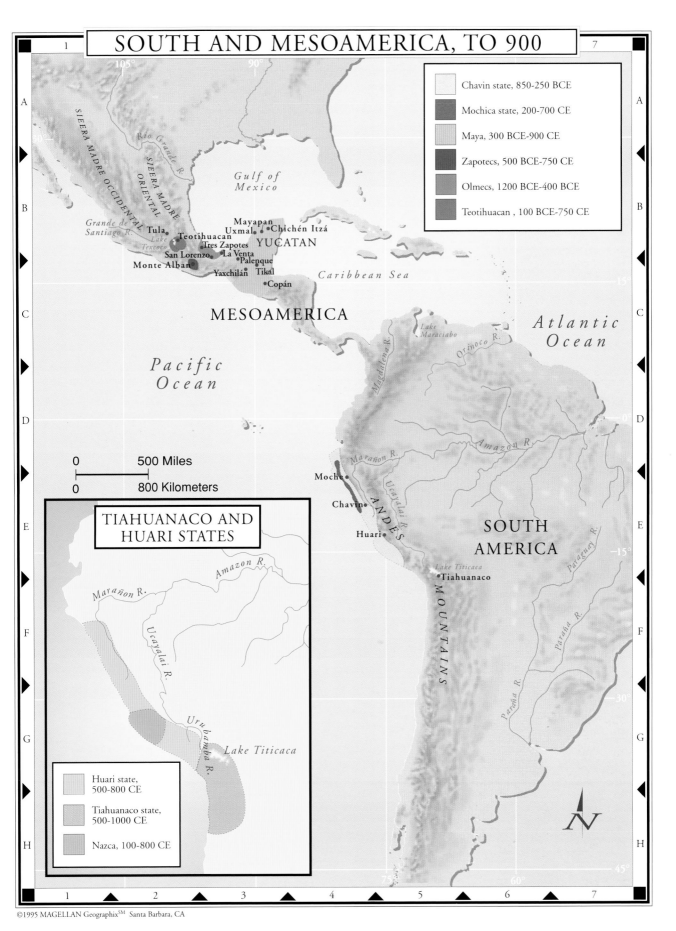

SIERRA MADRE OCCIDENTAL

SIERRA MADRE ORIENTAL

Rio Grande R.

Grande de Santiago R.

Gulf of Mexico

Lake Texcoco

Tula
Teotihuacan
Tres Zapotes
San Lorenzo
La Venta
Monte Albán
Yaxchilán

Mayapan
Uxmal
Chichén Itzá
YUCATAN
Palenque
Tikal
Copán

Caribbean Sea

MESOAMERICA

Pacific Ocean

Atlantic Ocean

Lake Maracaibo

Magdalena R.

Orinoco R.

Amazon R.

Marañon R.

Ucayalai R.

Moche

Chavin

Huari

ANDES

SOUTH AMERICA

Lake Titicaca
Tiahuanaco

MOUNTAINS

Paraguay R.

Paraná R.

Pilcomayo R.

Legend (top right):

- Chavin state, 850-250 BCE
- Mochica state, 200-700 CE
- Maya, 300 BCE-900 CE
- Zapotecs, 500 BCE-750 CE
- Olmecs, 1200 BCE-400 BCE
- Teotihuacan , 100 BCE-750 CE

Scale:

0 — 500 Miles
0 — 800 Kilometers

TIAHUANACO AND HUARI STATES

Amazon R.

Marañon R.

Ucayalai R.

Urubamba R.

Lake Titicaca

- Huari state, 500-800 CE
- Tiahuanaco state, 500-1000 CE
- Nazca, 100-800 CE

N

©1995 MAGELLAN Geographix℠ Santa Barbara, CA

THE CRUSADES

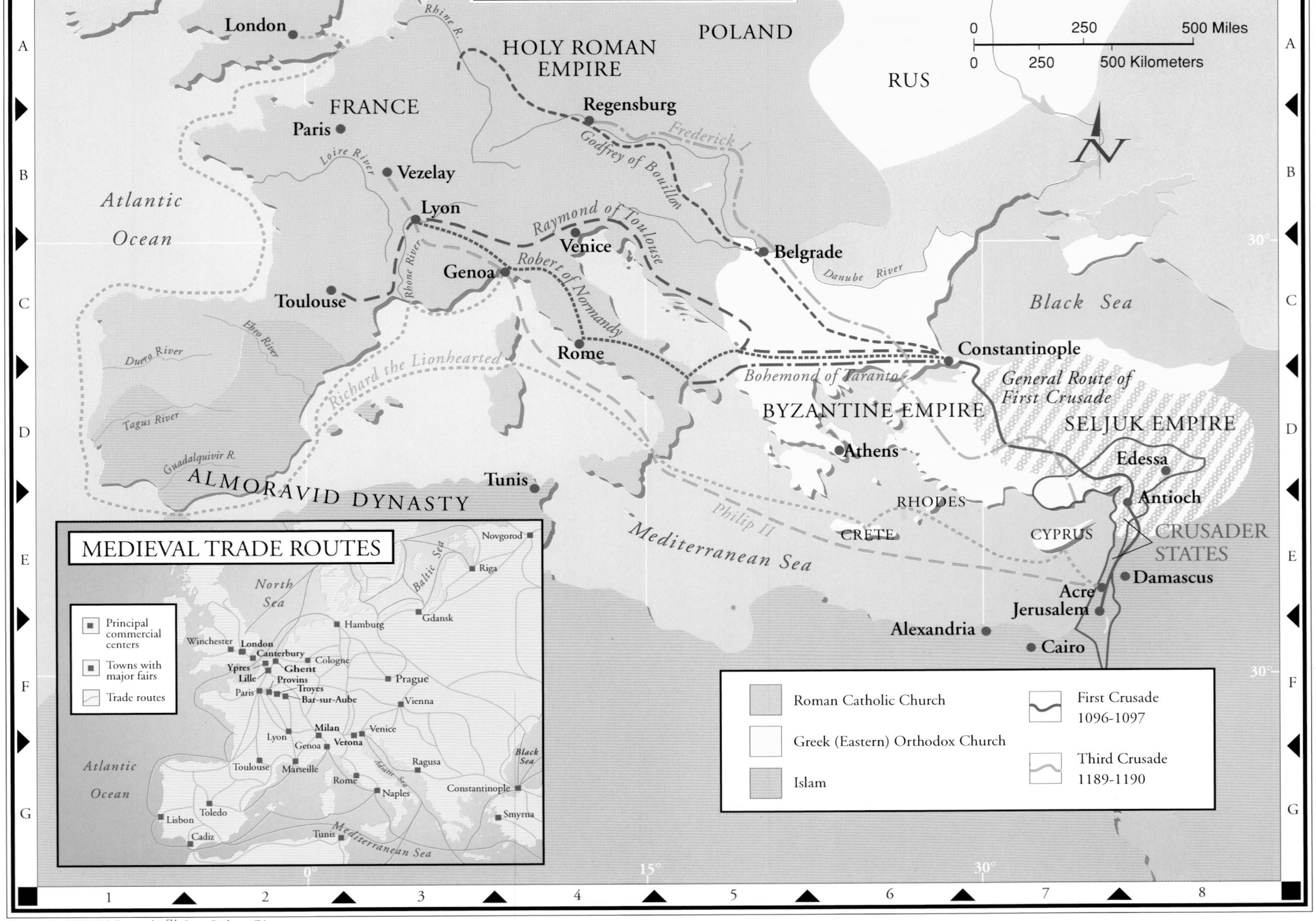

MEDIEVAL TRADE ROUTES

Legend:
- Principal commercial centers
- Towns with major fairs
- Trade routes

Inset map labels:
Atlantic Ocean, Lisbon, Cadiz, Toledo, Winchester, London, Canterbury, Cologne, Ypres, Ghent, Lille, Paris, Provins, Troyes, Bar-sur-Aube, Toulouse, Lyon, Genoa, Marseille, Milan, Verona, Venice, Rome, Naples, Ragusa, Constantinople, Smyrna, Hamburg, Prague, Vienna, Gdansk, Riga, Novgorod, North Sea, Baltic Sea, Black Sea, Mediterranean Sea, Rhine R., Rhône R.

Map labels:
Atlantic Ocean, London, Paris, FRANCE, Toulouse, Vezelay, Lyon, Genoa, Venice, Rome, HOLY ROMAN EMPIRE, POLAND, Regensburg, Belgrade, RUS, Black Sea, Tunis, Mediterranean Sea, BYZANTINE EMPIRE, Athens, CRETE, RHODES, Constantinople, CYPRUS, Alexandria, Jerusalem, Acre, Cairo, Damascus, Antioch, Edessa, CRUSADER STATES, SELJUK EMPIRE, ALMORAVID DYNASTY, Danube River, Tagus River, Duero River, Guadalquivir R., Ebro River, Loire River, Rhône River, Rhine R.

Route labels: Richard the Lionhearted, Raymond of Toulouse, Robert of Normandy, Godfrey of Bouillon, Frederick I, Bohemond of Taranto, General Route of First Crusade, Philip II

Legend:
- Roman Catholic Church
- Greek (Eastern) Orthodox Church
- Islam
- First Crusade 1096-1097
- Third Crusade 1189-1190

Scale: 0 250 500 Kilometers / 0 250 500 Miles

16

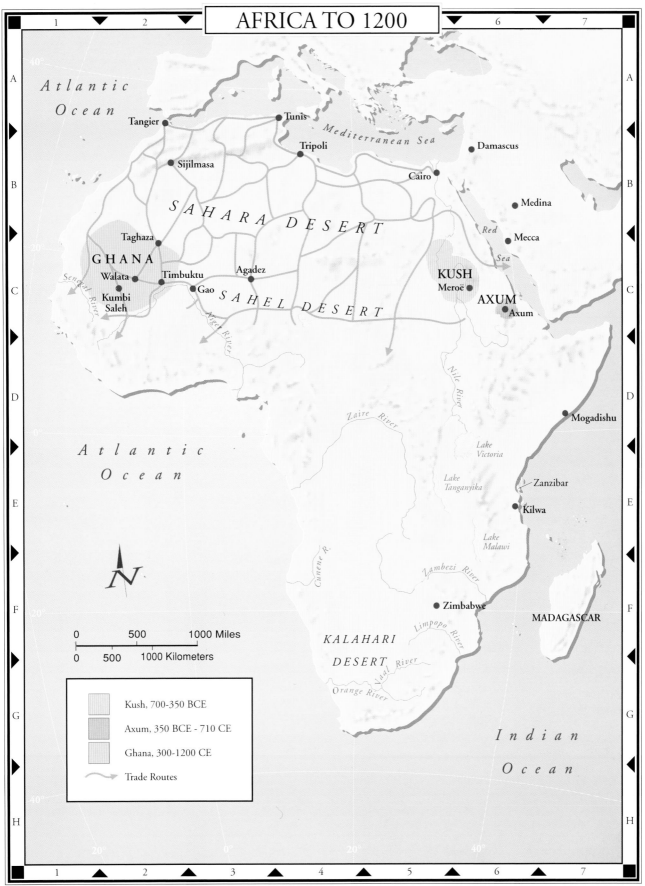

AFRICA TO 1200

Atlantic Ocean

Tangier

Tunis

Mediterranean Sea

Tripoli

Damascus

Sijilmasa

Cairo

S A H A R A   D E S E R T

Medina

Taghaza

Red

Mecca

GHANA

Walata

Timbuktu

Agadez

Sea

Kumbi Saleh

Gao

KUSH

Meroë

S A H E L   D E S E R T

AXUM

Axum

Senegal River

Niger River

Nile River

Atlantic Ocean

Zaire River

Mogadishu

Lake Victoria

Lake Tanganyika

Zanzibar

Kilwa

Lake Malawi

Cunene R.

Zambezi River

Zimbabwe

MADAGASCAR

Limpopo River

KALAHARI

DESERT

Vaal River

Indian Ocean

Orange River

0   500   1000 Miles

0   500   1000 Kilometers

Kush, 700-350 BCE

Axum, 350 BCE - 710 CE

Ghana, 300-1200 CE

Trade Routes

N

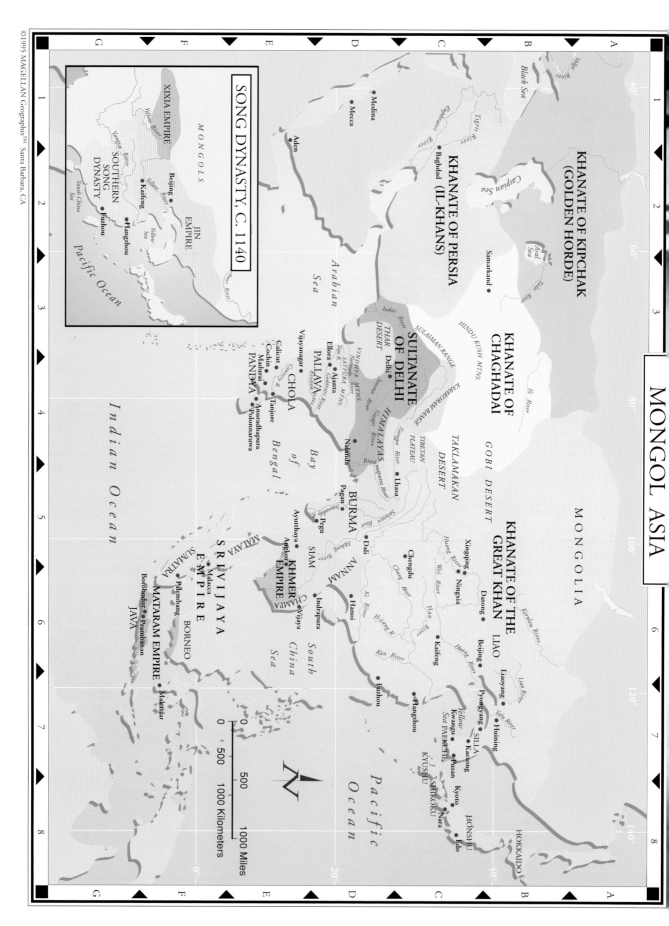

MONGOL ASIA

KHANATE OF KIPCHAK (GOLDEN HORDE)

KHANATE OF PERSIA (IL-KHANS)

KHANATE OF CHAGHADAI

KHANATE OF THE GREAT KHAN

SULTANATE OF DELHI

SONG DYNASTY, C. 1140

XIXIA EMPIRE

MONGOLS

SOUTHERN SONG DYNASTY

JIN EMPIRE

Beijing •
Kaifeng •
• Fuzhou
Hangzhou •

Yangtze River
Yellow River
Yellow River
South China Sea
Yellow Sea
Tatar River
Pacific Ocean

MONGOLIA

MONGOLS

Black Sea
Volga River
Caspian Sea
Aral Sea
Tatar River
Euphrates River
Tigris River
Ili River
Kerulen River

• Medina
• Mecca
• Aden
Baghdad •
Samarkand •

Arabian Sea

THAR DESERT
Delhi •
Nalanda •

HINDU KUSH MTNS
SULAIMAN RANGE
KARAKORAM RANGE
Indus River

TAKLAMAKAN DESERT

GOBI DESERT

LIAO

Huang River
Wei River
Han River
Chang River
Xi River
Hsiang R.
Kan River
Yalu River
Liao River

• Daong
• Xingqing
• Ningxia
Bejing •
• Chengdu
Kaifeng •
• Dali
Hangzhou •
• Fuzhou
• Liaoyang
Pyongyang •
Kwangu •
• Huining
• Kaesong
PAEKCHE
Pusan •
SILLA
KYUSHU
SHIKOKU
Kyoto •
Nara •
Edo •
HONSHU
HOKKAIDO

Yellow Sea

TIBETAN PLATEAU

Tsangpo River
Brahmaputra River
Ganges River
Yamuna River
Lhasa •

HIMALAYAS

VINDHYA MTNS
Narmada River
Tapi R.
SATPURA MTNS
Godavari River
Krishna River
Cavery R.

Ellora •
Ajanta •
PALLAVA
Vijayanagar •
Calicut •
Cochin •
Madurai •
PANDYA
Tanjore •
CHOLA
Anuradhapura •
Polonnaruwa •

Bay of Bengal

Indian Ocean

Pagan •
BURMA
Pegu •
Ayuthaya •
SIAM
Angkor •
KHMER EMPIRE
CHAMPA
Indrapura •
Vijaya •
Hanoi •
ANNAM

Irrawaddy R.
Salween River
Mekong River

MALAYA
SUMATRA
Malacca •
SRIVIJAYA EMPIRE
Palembang •
BORNEO
MATARAM EMPIRE
Borobodur • Prambanan
JAVA
Makassar •

South China Sea

Pacific Ocean

N

0   500   1000 Kilometers
0   500   1000 Miles

40°
60°
80°
100°
120°
140°
20°
0°

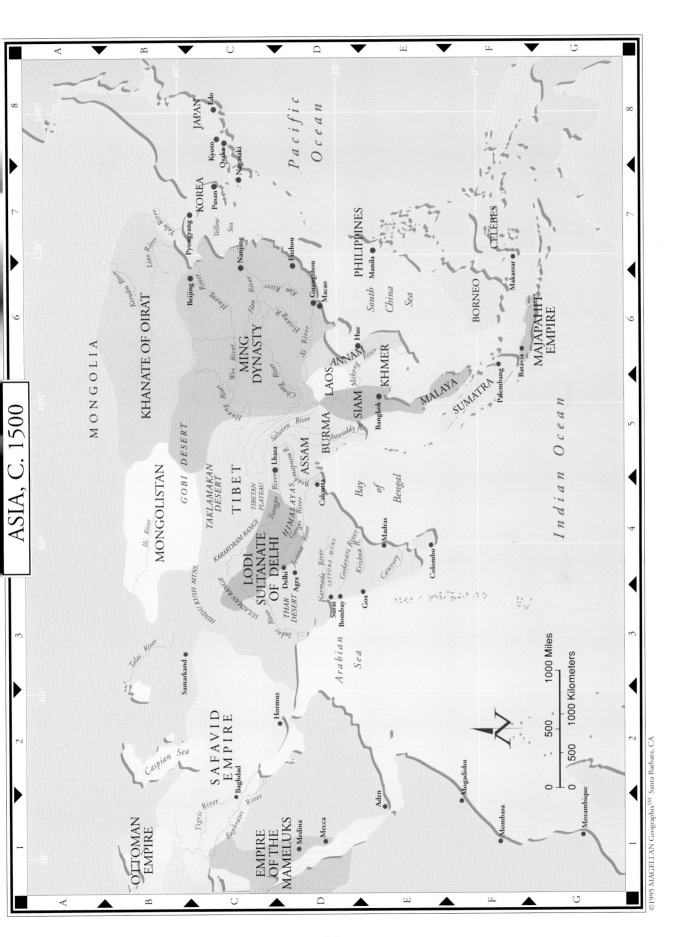

ASIA, C. 1500

OTTOMAN EMPIRE

SAFAVID EMPIRE

EMPIRE OF THE MAMELUKS

MONGOLIA

KHANATE OF OIRAT

MONGOLISTAN

GOBI DESERT

TAKLAMAKAN DESERT

TIBET

MING DYNASTY

KOREA

JAPAN

LODI SULTANATE OF DELHI

HIMALAYAS

ASSAM

BURMA

LAOS

ANNAM

SIAM

KHMER

MALAYA

SUMATRA

BORNEO

CELEBES

PHILIPPINES

MAJAPAHIT EMPIRE

Pacific Ocean

Indian Ocean

South China Sea

Yellow Sea

Bay of Bengal

Arabian Sea

Caspian Sea

Samarkand

Hormuz

Baghdad

Medina

Mecca

Aden

Mogadishu

Mombasa

Mozambique

Goa

Bombay

Surat

Delhi

Agra

Calcutta

Madras

Colombo

Lhasa

Beijing

Pyongyang

Pusan

Nanjing

Jinzhou

Guangzhou

Macao

Hue

Bangkok

Manila

Makassar

Batavia

Palembang

Kyoto

Osaka

Nagasaki

Edo

Tigris River

Euphrates River

Talas River

Ili River

Kerulen River

Amur River

Liao River

Yalu River

Hiang River

Wei River

Huang River

Han River

Hsiang R.

Kan River

Az River

Mekong River

Salween River

Irrawaddy R.

Tsangpo River

Brahmaputra R.

Ganges River

Jumna River

Narmada River

Indus River

Godavari River

Krishna R.

Cavery

Chang River

TIBETAN PLATEAU

HINDU KUSH MTNS.

KARAKORAM RANGE

SULAIMAN RANGE

THAR DESERT

SATPURA MTNS.

SULU

N

| 0 | 500 | 1000 Miles |
| 0 | 500 | 1000 Kilometers |

19

©1995 MAGELLAN Geographix℠ Santa Barbara, CA

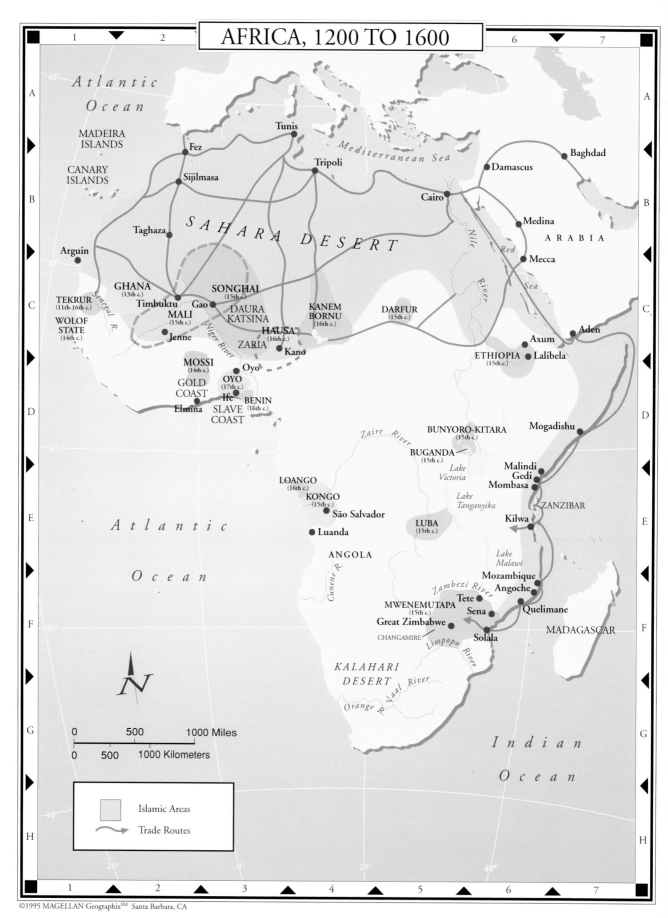

AFRICA, 1200 TO 1600

Atlantic Ocean

MADEIRA ISLANDS

CANARY ISLANDS

Tunis

Fez

Sijilmasa

Mediterranean Sea

Tripoli

Baghdad

Damascus

Cairo

Taghaza

S A H A R A   D E S E R T

Arguin

GHANA
(13th c.)

Timbuktu Gao

SONGHAI
(15th c.)

DAURA
KATSINA

Medina

ARABIA

Mecca

Red Sea

Nile River

TEKRUR
(11th-16th c.)

MALI
(15th c.)

Senegal R.

Jenne

Niger River

HAUSA
(16th c.)

ZARIA

Kano

KANEM
BORNU
(16th c.)

DARFUR
(15th c.)

Axum

Aden

WOLOF
STATE
(14th c.)

MOSSI
(14th c.)

Oyo

GOLD
COAST

OYO
(17th c.)

Ife

Elmina

SLAVE
COAST

BENIN
(16th c.)

ETHIOPIA
(15th c.)

Lalibela

Zaire River

BUNYORO-KITARA
(15th c.)

BUGANDA
(15th c.)

Mogadishu

LOANGO
(16th c.)

*Lake
Victoria*

Malindi
Gedi
Mombasa

KONGO
(15th c.)

São Salvador

Luanda

*Lake
Tanganyika*

LUBA
(15th c.)

ZANZIBAR

Kilwa

Atlantic Ocean

ANGOLA

Cunene R.

*Lake
Malawi*

Mozambique
Angoche

Zambezi River

MWENEMUTAPA
(15th c.)

Tete

Sena

Quelimane

Great Zimbabwe

CHANGAMIRE

Solala

Limpopo River

MADAGASCAR

*KALAHARI
DESERT*

Orange R. *Vaal River*

Indian Ocean

0   500   1000 Miles

0   500   1000 Kilometers

N

Islamic Areas

Trade Routes

©1995 MAGELLAN Geographix^SM Santa Barbara, CA

Gulf of Mexico

Atlantic Ocean

Grande de Santiago R.

Tula
Tenochtitlan • Teotihuacan
Lake Texcoco
Oaxaca •

Uxmal • • Chichén Itzá
YUCATAN
• Tikal
• Copán

Caribbean Sea

MESOAMERICA

Magdalena River
Orinoco River

• Quito

Pacific Ocean

Marañon River
Amazon River

ANDES

Ucayali River

SOUTH AMERICA

Machu Picchu •
Cuzco •
• Pucará de Andalgala
Lake Titicaca
• Tiahuanaco

MOUNTAINS

Coquimbu •

Santiago •

N

	Tiahuanaco state, 500-1000
	Chimu state, 800-1465
	Inca Empire, 1438-1532
	Toltec Empire, 900-1200
	Teotihuacan Empire, 100 BCE-750 CE
	Aztec Empire, 1325-1521

0	500 Miles
0	800 Kilometers

EUROPE, 1560

Legend

- Spanish Hapsburgs
- Austrian Hapsburgs
- Boundary of the Holy Roman Empire

Scale

0 250 500 Kilometers
0 250 500 Miles

15°
0°
15°
30°
45°

N

Atlantic Ocean

IRELAND
Dublin

SCOTLAND

ENGLAND
York
London
Plymouth
Cherbourg
Brest

North Sea

NORWAY AND DENMARK
Oslo
Copenhagen

SWEDEN
Stockholm

Baltic Sea

LIVONIA
Konigsberg
Danzig
Minsk

LITHUANIA

POLAND
Warsaw

Kiev

KHANATE OF THE CRIMEA

Dnepr River
Don River
Volga River

BESSARABIA

MOLDAVIA
WALLACHIA
Bucharest

TRANSILVANIA

HUNGARY
Pest

AUSTRIAN MONARCHY
Vienna
Prague

SAXONY
Berlin
BRANDENBURG
Frankfurt
Cologne
Hamburg
Munich
Metz

NETHERLANDS
Antwerp
Utrech

FRANCE
Paris
Nantes
Bordeaux
Toulouse
Marseille
Avignon

Seine River
Loire R.
Rhone R.
Rhine R.
Elbe R.
Vistula River
Danube River
Po River
Tigris River
Euphrates River

SWITZERLAND
FRENCH COMTE
SAVOY
MILAN
GENOA
Genoa
Tuscan
MODENA
Florence
TUSCANY
PAPAL STATES
Rome
VENETIAN REPUBLIC
Venice

CORSICA
SARDINA
SICILY
Palermo

NAPLES AND SICILY
Naples

Adriatic Sea
Mediterranean Sea

MONTENEGRO

Athens

CRETE (Ven.)
CYPRUS (Ven.)

OTTOMAN EMPIRE
Istanbul

Black Sea

Acre
Damascus

Caspian Sea

SPAIN
Lisbon
Oporto
PORTUGAL
Seville
Granada
Valencia
Barcelona

Duero R.
Tagus R.
Guadalquivir R.

Tanger (Sp.)
FEZ AND MOROCCO
Oran (Sp.)
ALGERIA
Tunis (Sp.)

ITALY, 1494

HOLY ROMAN EMPIRE

SWISS CONFEDERATION

SALUZZO
SAVOY
MILAN
Milan
MANTUA
MANTUAN REPUBLIC
Ferrara
MODENA
GENOA
Genoa
FLORENCE
Florence
SIENA
PAPAL STATES
Ravenna
Rome
Venice
VENETIAN REPUBLIC

KINGDOM OF SARDINIA

CORSICA (GENOA)

KINGDOM OF THE TWO SICILIES
Naples
Salerno
Bari
Palermo

Ragusa

Mediterranean Sea
Adriatic Sea

OTTOMAN EMPIRE

22

EUROPE, 1648

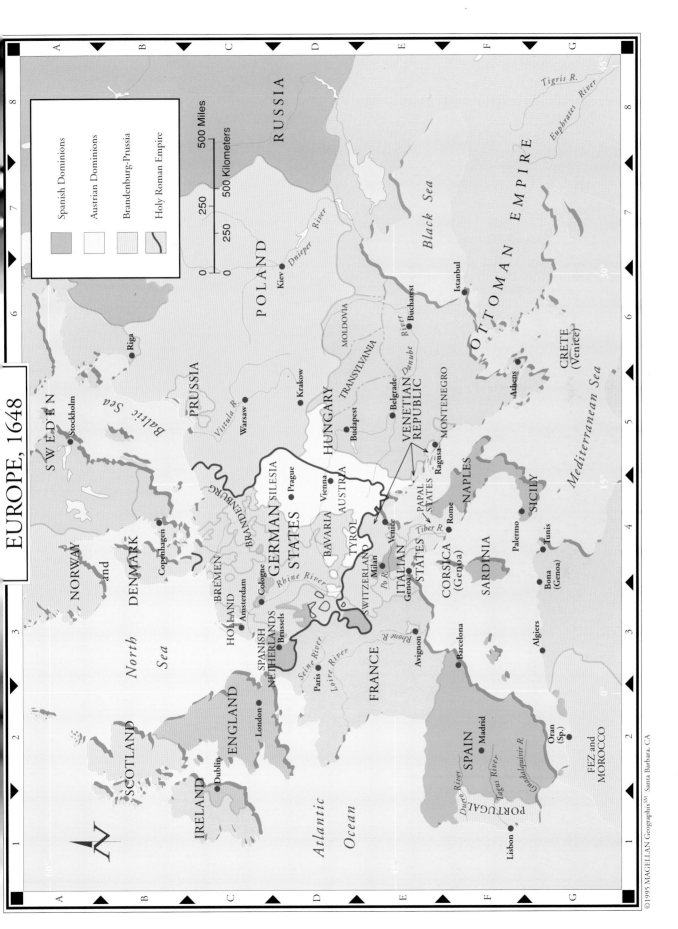

Legend:
- Spanish Dominions
- Austrian Dominions
- Brandenburg-Prussia
- Holy Roman Empire

500 Miles

500 Kilometers

| 0 | 250 | 500 |
| 0 | 250 | 500 |

N

RUSSIA

POLAND

Kiev

Dnieper River

Riga

PRUSSIA

Vistula R.

Warsaw

Krakow

HUNGARY

Budapest

TRANSYLVANIA

MOLDOVIA

Belgrade

Danube River

Bucharest

Black Sea

Istanbul

OTTOMAN EMPIRE

Tigris R.

Euphrates River

SWEDEN

Stockholm

Baltic Sea

SILESIA

Prague

GERMAN STATES

BRANDENBURG

Vienna

AUSTRIA

BAVARIA

TYROL

VENETIAN REPUBLIC

MONTENEGRO

Ragusa

Athens

CRETE (Venice)

Mediterranean Sea

NORWAY and DENMARK

Copenhagen

BREMEN

HOLLAND

Amsterdam

Cologne

Rhine River

SWITZERLAND

Milan

Po R.

Venice

PAPAL STATES

Rome

Tiber R.

ITALIAN STATES

Genoa

CORSICA (Genoa)

NAPLES

SARDINIA

Palermo

SICILY

Tunis

Bona (Genoa)

North Sea

SCOTLAND

ENGLAND

London

IRELAND

Dublin

SPANISH NETHERLANDS

Brussels

Paris

Seine River

Loire River

Rhone R.

FRANCE

Avignon

Barcelona

Algiers

Atlantic Ocean

SPAIN

Madrid

Oran (Sp.)

FEZ and MOROCCO

Duero River

Tagus River

Guadalquivir R.

PORTUGAL

Lisbon

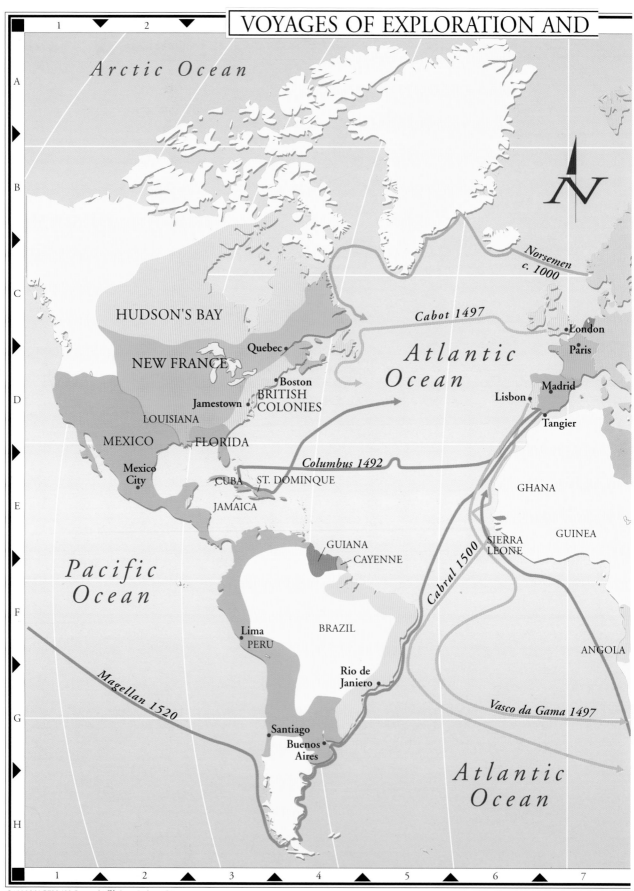

Arctic Ocean

A

N

B

Norsemen c. 1000

C

HUDSON'S BAY

Cabot 1497

London

Paris

Atlantic Ocean

Quebec

NEW FRANCE

Boston

Madrid

Lisbon

D

Jamestown

BRITISH COLONIES

Tangier

LOUISIANA

MEXICO

FLORIDA

Mexico City

Columbus 1492

GHANA

CUBA

ST. DOMINQUE

E

JAMAICA

GUINEA

SIERRA LEONE

Pacific Ocean

GUIANA

CAYENNE

Cabral 1500

F

BRAZIL

Lima

PERU

ANGOLA

Rio de Janiero

Magellan 1520

Vasco da Gama 1497

G

Santiago

Buenos Aires

Atlantic Ocean

H

12   13   14

Arctic Ocean

	British empire
	French empire
	Spanish empire
	Dutch empire
	Portuguese empire

RUSSIA

Moscow

SIBERIA

A

B

C

Istanbul

OTTOMAN
EMPIRE

PERSIA

Ormuz (Br.)

TIBET

CHINA

KOREA   JAPAN
Kyoto
Nagasaki

D

INDIA

Bombay
Goa
(Port.)

Circas (Fr.)
Madras (Br.)

CEYLON

Canton

Fuzhou

Macao
(Port.)

Manila

PHILIPPINES

*Pacific
Ocean*

Magellan 1521

E

MALAYA

SUMATRA   *BORNEO*   *CELEBES*
DUTCH EAST INDIES
JAVA
Timor

Zanzibar

*Indian
Ocean*

Mozambique

F

MADAGASCAR

El Cano 1522

AUSTRALIA

G

CAPE OF
GOOD HOPE

H

8   9   10   11   12   13   14

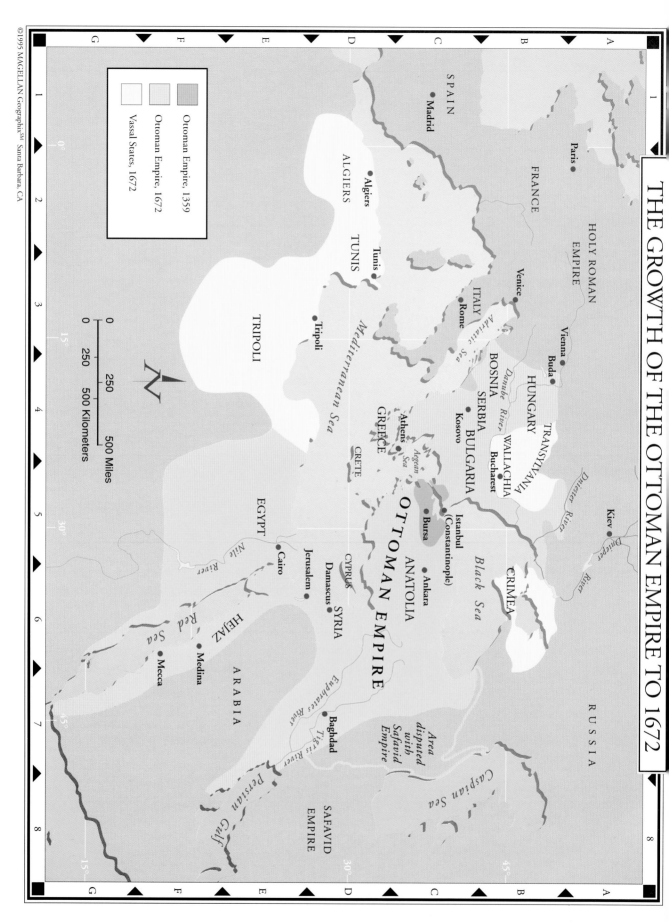

THE GROWTH OF THE OTTOMAN EMPIRE TO 1672

Ottoman Empire, 1359
Ottoman Empire, 1672
Vassal States, 1672

©1995 MAGELLAN Geographix℠ Santa Barbara, CA

N

0 250 500 Kilometers
0 250 500 Miles

SPAIN
Madrid
Paris
FRANCE
HOLY ROMAN EMPIRE
ALGIERS
Algiers
TUNIS
Tunis
TRIPOLI
Tripoli
Mediterranean Sea
Venice
ITALY
Rome
Adriatic Sea
Vienna
Buda
HUNGARY
TRANSYLVANIA
BOSNIA
SERBIA
Kosovo
BULGARIA
Bucharest
WALLACHIA
Danube River
Dniester River
Dnieper River
Kiev
RUSSIA
CRIMEA
Black Sea
GREECE
Athens
Aegean Sea
CRETE
Istanbul (Constantinople)
Bursa
ANATOLIA
Ankara
OTTOMAN EMPIRE
CYPRUS
Damascus
SYRIA
Jerusalem
Cairo
EGYPT
Nile River
Red Sea
HEJAZ
Medina
Mecca
ARABIA
Euphrates River
Tigris River
Baghdad
Area disputed with Safavid Empire
Persian Gulf
Caspian Sea
SAFAVID EMPIRE

0°
15°
30°
45°
15°
30°
45°

AFRICAN SLAVE TRADE

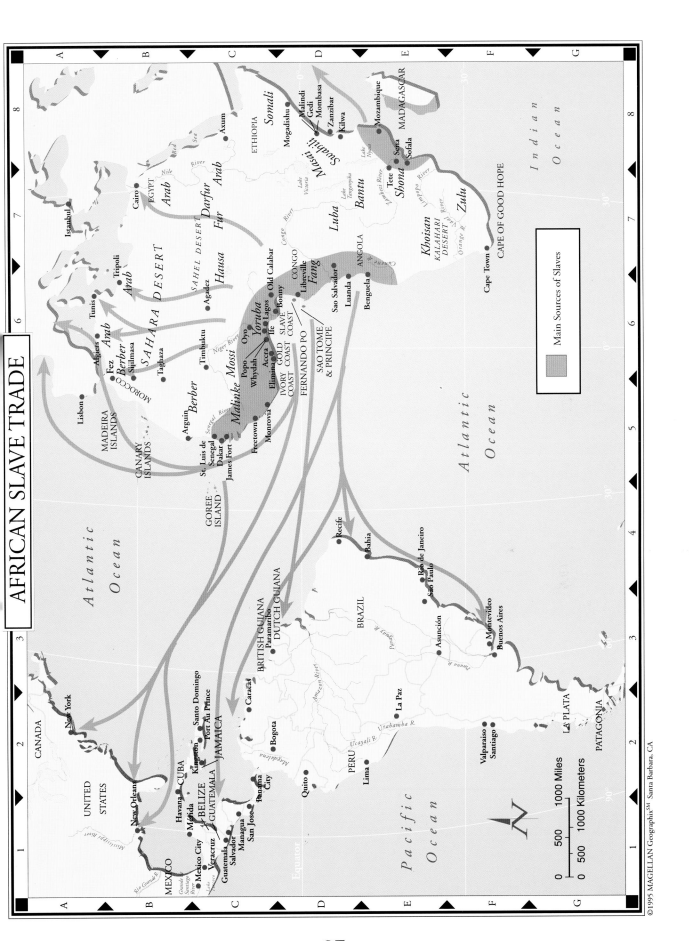

Main Sources of Slaves

©1995 MAGELLAN Geographix℠ Santa Barbara, CA

EUROPE, 1714

Legend:
- Holy Roman Empire
- Hapsburg Dominions
- Bourbon Dominions

Scale:
0 — 200 — 400 Kilometers
0 — 200 — 400 Miles

N

Atlantic Ocean

North Sea

Baltic Sea

Mediterranean Sea

Adriatic Sea

45°
15°
0°
30°

Countries and Regions

FEZ and MOROCCO
ALGERIA
TUNIS
PORTUGAL
SPAIN
GREAT BRITAIN
FRANCE
AUSTRIAN NETHERLANDS
UNITED NETHERLANDS
DENMARK and NORWAY
SWEDEN
LITHUANIA
POLAND
PRUSSIA
Hanover
Saxony
Bavaria
SWITZERLAND
Lorraine
AVIGNON
GENOA
Piedmont
Milan
Parma
Modena
Tuscany States
PAPAL STATES
KINGDOM OF NAPLES
Republic of Venice
CORSICA (Genoa)
SARDINIA (Austria)
SICILY (Savoy)
MOREA (Venice)
KINGDOM OF HUNGARY
OTTOMAN EMPIRE

Cities

Lisbon
Gibraltar (Gr. Br.)
Madrid
Barcelona
Marseilles
Dublin
London
Paris
Amsterdam
Cologne
Hamburg
Berlin
Frankfurt
Dresden
Prague
Munich
Vienna
Buda
Pest
Belgrade
Ragusa
Rome
Venice
Warsaw
Danzig
Riga
Kiev
Bucharest
Athens
Istanbul

Rivers

Guadalquivir R.
Tagus River
Duero River
Loire R.
Seine R.
Rhone R.
Rhine R.
Elbe R.
Po River
Tiber R.
Danube River
Vistula River

THE GROWTH OF RUSSIA

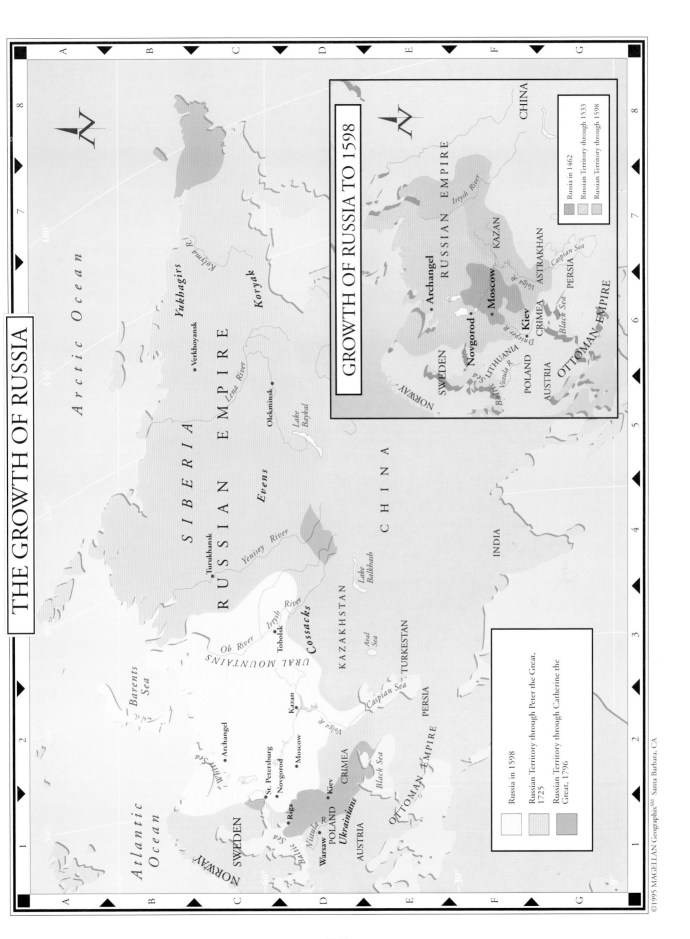

GROWTH OF RUSSIA TO 1598

Inset map legend:
- Russia in 1462
- Russian Territory through 1533
- Russian Territory through 1598

Inset map labels:
Arctic Ocean · CHINA · RUSSIAN EMPIRE · Irtysh River · KAZAN · Archangel · Moscow · Novgorod · Kiev · ASTRAKHAN · Caspian Sea · Volga R. · CRIMEA · Black Sea · PERSIA · Dnieper R. · SWEDEN · NORWAY · LITHUANIA · POLAND · AUSTRIA · OTTOMAN EMPIRE · Baltic Sea · Vistula R.

Main map legend:
- Russia in 1598
- Russian Territory through Peter the Great, 1725
- Russian Territory through Catherine the Great, 1796

Main map labels:
Atlantic Ocean · Arctic Ocean · Barents Sea · Kolyma R. · Yukhagirs · Koryak · Verkhoyansk · Lena River · SIBERIA · RUSSIAN EMPIRE · Evens · Olekminsk · Lake Baikal · Yenisey River · Turukhansk · CHINA · Irtysh River · Ob River · Tobolsk · Cossacks · URAL MOUNTAINS · KAZAKHSTAN · Lake Balkhash · Aral Sea · TURKESTAN · Kazan · Volga R. · Caspian Sea · PERSIA · White Sea · Archangel · Moscow · St. Petersburg · Novgorod · Kiev · CRIMEA · Black Sea · OTTOMAN EMPIRE · Riga · Baltic Sea · Warsaw · Vistula R. · POLAND · Ukrainians · AUSTRIA · SWEDEN · NORWAY · INDIA

ASIA, 1800

Legend

- Area under British Control
- Area under Dutch Control
- Area under Spanish Control

Places and Features

RUSSIA

Syr Darya River

Ili River

Ormuz

Samarkand

AFGHANISTAN

XINJIANG

HINDU KUSH MTNS

KARAKORUM

SULAIMAN RANGE

Indus River

Arabian Sea

Bombay

Goa (Port.)

Surat

THAR DESERT

Narmada River

Godavari River

Krishna R.

Cauvery R.

DECCAN PLATEAU

Colombo

Madras

INDIA

Delhi

Agra

Yamuna R.

Ganges River

Calcutta

BENGAL

Dacca

Brahmaputra R.

TIBET

Lhasa

TIBETAN PLATEAU

HIMALAYAS

Tsangpo River

Salween River

Mekong River

Irrawaddy R.

TAKLAMAKAN DESERT

GANSU

GOBI DESERT

MONGOLIA

Kerulen River

INNER MONGOLIA

HEILONGJIANG

JILIN

Great Wall

Beijing

ZHILI

SHENJING

Liao River

Yalu R.

KOREA

Pyongyang

SHANDONG

Yellow Sea

SHANXI

SHAANXI

HENAN

HUBEI

Han River

Huang R.

Wei River

Grand Canal

Kan R.

ANHUI

JIANGSU

ZHEJIANG

Shanghai

JIANGXI

FUJIAN

Fuzhou

TAIWAN (FORMOSA)

GUANGDONG

Guangzhou

Macao (Port.)

GUANGXI

GUIZHOU

HUNAN

SICHUAN

Yangzi River

Xi River

Xi River

Yi River

Huang River

YUNNAN

CHINA

Bay of Bengal

BURMA

Rangoon

Ava

Bangkok

SIAM

LAOS

CAMBODIA

Hanoi

ANNAM

Binh Dinh

Saigon

South China Sea

PHILIPPINES

Manila

SUMATRA

Palembang

Singapore

Batavia

JAVA

DUTCH EAST INDIES

BORNEO

CELEBES

Makassar

NEW GUINEA

Indian Ocean

Pacific Ocean

JAPAN

Nagasaki

Kyoto

Osaka

Edo

Scale

0 500 1000 Kilometers

0 500 1000 Miles

N

60° 80° 100° 120° 140°

0° 20° 40°

UNITED STATES

Atlantic Ocean

MEXICO
(1821)

Gulf of Mexico

Rio Grande R.

Mississippi River

Grande de Santiago R.

Vera Cruz

Mexico City

Lake Texcoco

British Honduras (Br.)

Havana **Cuba (Sp.)** **Haiti** **Santo Domingo**

Jamaica (Br.) **Puerto Rico (Sp.)**

Virgin Islands (Den.)

Guatemala (1839) Guatemala

El Salvador (1839)

Nicaragua (1839)

Tegucigalapa

Managua

Belice

Honduras (1839)

Caribbean Sea

Curacao (Dutch)

Caracus

Trinidad (Br.)

British Guiana

San Jose

San Salvador

Costa Rica (1839)

Panama

Venezuela
(1829)

Georgetown

Dutch Guiana

French Guiana

Paramaribo

Cayenne

Magdalena R.

Bogota

Colombia
(1819)

Pacific Ocean

Quito

Ecuador
(1822)

Equator

Amazon River

Ucayali R.

Peru
(1821)

Lima

Urubamba R.

La Paz

Bolivia
(1825)

Lake Titicaca

Brazil
(Monarchy 1822-1889;
Republic 1889)

Recife

Bahia

Paraguay R.

Paraguay
(1811)

Rio de Janeiro

Chile

Asunción

Panama R.

Valparaiso

Santiago

Argentina
(1816)

Buenos Aires

Uruguay
(1828)

Montevideo

| 0 | 500 | 1000 Miles |
| 0 | 800 | 1600 Kilometers |

Falkland Islands (Br.)

EUROPE, 1815

Boundary of the
German Confederation

Map labels

PORTUGAL
Lisbon
SPAIN
Madrid
Tagus R.
Duero R.
Guadalquivir R.

MOROCCO
ALGERIA

Atlantic
Ocean

UNITED KINGDOM
Dublin
London

FRANCE
Paris
Marseilles
Seine R.
Loire R.
Rhône R.

SWITZERLAND

KINGDOM OF
SARDINIA
KINGDOM OF
TUSCANY
PARMA
MODENA
LOMBARDY
Milan
PAPAL
STATES
Rome
KINGDOM OF
THE TWO
SICILIES
Naples

NETHERLANDS
Amsterdam
Cologne
Rhine R.
Hanover
Württemberg
Hesse
Bavaria
Munich
Prague
Vienna
Buda
Danube River

AUSTRIAN EMPIRE

DENMARK
Copenhagen
Schleswig
Holstein
Hamburg

North
Sea

NORWAY
SWEDEN

Prussia
Berlin
Warsaw
Vistula R.

Baltic Sea

Belgrade
Athens

OTTOMAN EMPIRE
Istanbul

RUSSIA
Odessa
St. Petersburg

Black Sea

Mediterranean Sea

Euphrates River
Tigris River
Volga River

Adriatic Sea

N

45°
60°
0°
15°
30°

0 250 500 Kilometers
0 250 500 Miles

NAPOLEON'S EMPIRE

UNITED
KINGDOM
London

FRANCE
Paris
Waterloo, June 18, 1815
Jena, 1806

CONFEDERATION
OF THE
RHINE
Ulm, 1805
Leipzig, October 16-19, 1813
Austerlitz, December 2, 1805

HELVETIA
ITALY
Rome
CORSICA
SARDINIA
SICILY
NAPLES

SPAIN

KINGDOM OF
SWEDEN
NORWAY AND

NORWAY

DENMARK
Berlin
PRUSSIA
WARSAW
Tilsit, 1807
Invasion of
Russia June, 1812
Moscow

AUSTRIA

OTTOMAN
EMPIRE

RUSSIA
St. Petersburg

North
Sea
Baltic Sea
Black Sea

Mediterranean Sea
Adriatic Sea

France in 1799
Napoleon's additions
to France, 1812
States under Napoleon's
control, 1812
Napoleon's allies, 1812

0 250 500 Kilometers
0 250 500 Miles

Boundary of the German
Confederation of 1815

Prussia, 1866

German Empire, 1866

Ceded by France, 1871

100   200 Miles

100   200 Kilometers

N

SWEDEN

DENMARK

North Sea

Baltic Sea

55°

SCHLESWIG

HOLSTEIN

EAST PRUSSIA

Danzig

WEST PRUSSIA

MECKLENBURG

POMERANIA

Hamburg

OLDENBURG

HANOVER

BRANDENBURG

POSEN

Vistula River

RUSSIA

Berlin

Spree R.

Warta River

Warsaw

NETHERLANDS

Rhine River

WESTPHALIA

Ruhr River

HESSE

Dresden

Oder River

Cologne

SILESIA

BELGIUM

NASSAU

THURINGIA

SAXONY

Elbe River

Main R.

Prague

DARMSTADT

BARVARIAN
PALATINATE

BAVARIA

AUSTRIA

LORRAINE

HUNGARY

BADEN

WURTTEMBERG

Danube River

Vienna

ALSACE

Munich

FRANCE

HOHENZOLLERN

SWITZERLAND

45°

ITALY

OTTOMAN EMPIRE

5°   15°   25°

Kingdom of Sardinia, 1859

Annexations by Sardinia, 1859

Annexations by Sardinia, 1860
establishment of the Kingdom of Italy

To Kingdom of Italy, 1866

To Kingdom of Italy, 1870

AUSTRIA - HUNGARY

FRANCE

SWITZERLAND

TYROL

SAVOY
(to France,
1860)

PIEDMONT

LOMBARDY

VENETIA

Milan

Venice

Trieste

Turin

Po River

PARMA

MODENA

Genoa

Bologna

OTTOMAN
EMPIRE

NICE
(to France,
1860)

Florence

TUSCANY

Ancona

Zara

Tiber River

Adriatic Sea

KINGDOM
OF
SARDINIA

CORSICA

PAPAL
STATES

Ragusa

Rome

Bari

Naples

SARDINIA

Tyrrhenian
Sea

KINGDOM

OF THE

TWO SICILIES

N

Messina

Palermo

SICILY

0   50   100 Miles

0   50   100 Kilometers

Mediterranean Sea

INDUSTRIALIZATION IN EUROPE

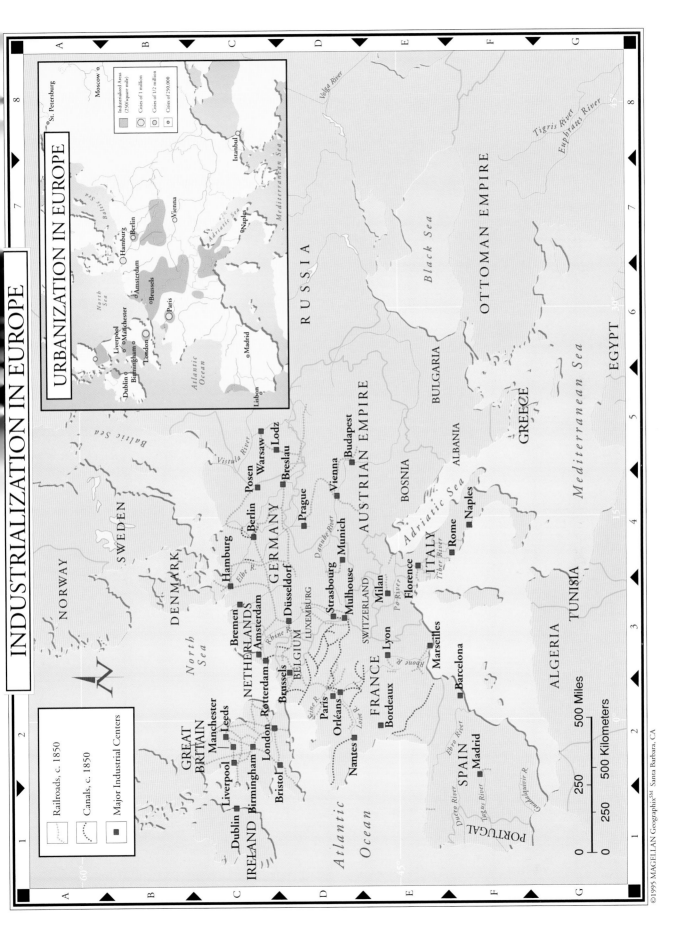

URBANIZATION IN EUROPE

Industrialized Areas (250/square mile)
- ○ Cities of 1 million
- ◎ Cities of 1/2 million
- ▫ Cities of 250,000

St. Petersburg
Moscow
Istanbul
Vienna
Naples
Hamburg
Berlin
Amsterdam
Brussels
Paris
Liverpool
Manchester
Birmingham
London
Dublin
Madrid
Lisbon

North Sea
Atlantic Ocean
Baltic Sea
Adriatic Sea
Mediterranean Sea

Railroads, c. 1850
Canals, c. 1850
■ Major Industrial Centers

NORWAY
SWEDEN
DENMARK
GREAT BRITAIN
IRELAND
Dublin
Liverpool
Manchester
Leeds
Birmingham
Bristol
London
NETHERLANDS
Amsterdam
Rotterdam
Bremen
Hamburg
BELGIUM
Brussels
LUXEMBURG
Düsseldorf
GERMANY
Berlin
Posen
Warsaw
Lodz
Breslau
Prague
Vienna
Budapest
AUSTRIAN EMPIRE
Munich
Strasbourg
Mulhouse
SWITZERLAND
FRANCE
Paris
Orléans
Nantes
Bordeaux
Lyon
Marseilles
Barcelona
Madrid
SPAIN
PORTUGAL
Milan
Florence
ITALY
Rome
Naples
BOSNIA
BULGARIA
ALBANIA
GREECE
ALGERIA
TUNISIA
EGYPT
OTTOMAN EMPIRE
RUSSIA
Black Sea
Mediterranean Sea
Adriatic Sea
North Sea
Baltic Sea
Atlantic Ocean

Vistula River
Volga River
Danube River
Elbe R.
Rhine R.
Seine R.
Loire R.
Rhône R.
Po River
Tiber River
Ebro River
Duero River
Tagus River
Guadalquivir R.
Tigris River
Euphrates River

500 Miles
500 Kilometers
0   250   500
0   250   500

©1995 MAGELLAN Geographix℠ Santa Barbara, CA

35

WORLD IMPERIALISM, 1900

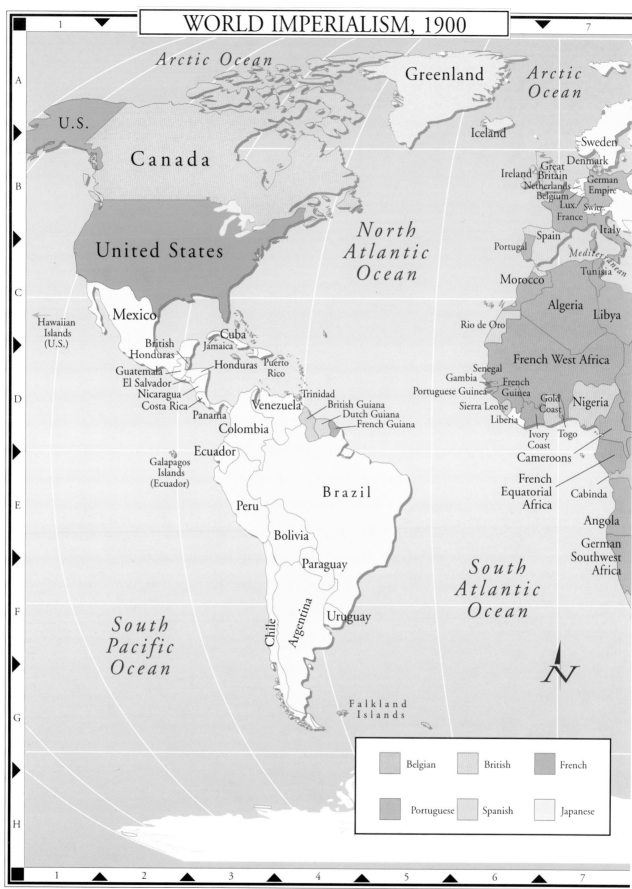

Arctic Ocean

Greenland

Arctic Ocean

U.S.

Canada

Iceland

Sweden
Denmark
Ireland Great Britain
Netherlands German Empire
Belgium
Lux. Switz.
France
Italy

United States

North Atlantic Ocean

Spain
Portugal
Mediterranean
Tunisia
Morocco

Mexico

Hawaiian Islands (U.S.)

Cuba
Jamaica
British Honduras
Honduras Puerto Rico
Guatemala
El Salvador
Nicaragua
Costa Rica
Panama
Trinidad
Venezuela British Guiana
Dutch Guiana
French Guiana
Colombia

Rio de Oro

Algeria Libya

French West Africa

Senegal
Gambia
Portuguese Guinea French Guinea
Sierra Leone Gold Coast Nigeria
Liberia
Ivory Coast Togo

Ecuador

Galapagos Islands (Ecuador)

Cameroons

French Equatorial Africa Cabinda

Brazil

Peru

Angola

German Southwest Africa

Bolivia

Paraguay

South Atlantic Ocean

South Pacific Ocean

Chile Argentina Uruguay

Falkland Islands

N

	Belgian		British		French
	Portuguese		Spanish		Japanese

36

A

B

Arctic Ocean

R u s s i a

Austria-
Hungary

Albania

Bulgaria

Ottoman

Greece

Sea

Empire

Persia

Afghanistan

C h i n a

Korea

Japan

*North
Pacific
Ocean*

Libya

Egypt

Arabia

Nepal

Bhutan

I n d i a

Burma

Taiwan

C

Anglo-
Egyptian
Sudan

Eritrea

French
Somaliland

*Arabian
Sea*

*Bay of
Bengal*

Siam

French
Indochina

Philippines

French
Equatorial
Africa

Ethiopia

British
Somaliland

Italian
Somaliland

Malaysia

Pacific Islands
(German, 1899)

D

Uganda

British East
Africa

Singapore

Belgian
Congo

German East
Africa

D u t c h   E a s t   I n d i e s

Papua
New Guinea

Angola

Nyasaland

E

Rhodesia

Mozambique

Madagascar

*Indian
Ocean*

A u s t r a l i a

Bechuanaland

Swaziland

South
Africa

Basutoland

F

New
Zealand

G

	American		German		Italian
	Dutch		Danish		Independent

H

©1995 MAGELLAN Geographix^SM Santa Barbara, CA

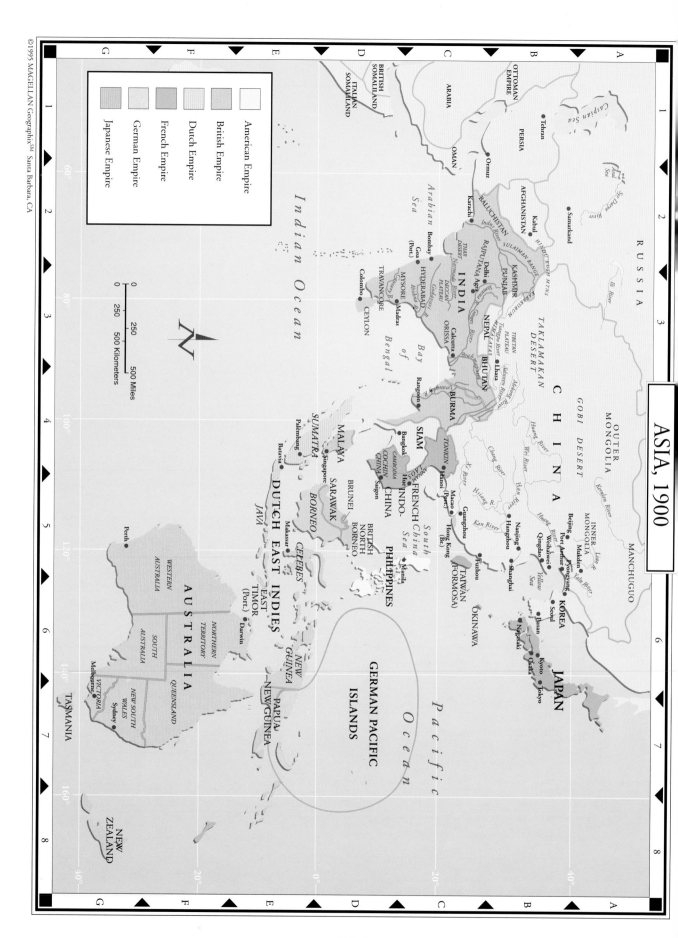

ASIA, 1900

Legend:
- American Empire
- British Empire
- Dutch Empire
- French Empire
- German Empire
- Japanese Empire

N

0 250 500 Miles
0 250 500 Kilometers

RUSSIA

OTTOMAN EMPIRE
ARABIA
PERSIA
OMAN
AFGHANISTAN
BALUCHISTAN
Tehran
Samarkand
Kabul
Karachi
Ormuz

BRITISH SOMALILAND
ITALIAN SOMALILAND

Indian Ocean
Arabian Sea

CHINA
OUTER MONGOLIA
INNER MONGOLIA
MANCHUGUO
GOBI DESERT
TAKLAMAKAN DESERT

INDIA
KASHMIR
PUNJAB
Delhi
Agra
RAJPUTANA
NEPAL
BHUTAN
HYDERABAD
MYSORE
TRAVANCORE
ORISSA
Calcutta
Madras
Bombay
Goa (Port.)
Colombo
CEYLON
DECCAN PLATEAU
THAR DESERT
TIBETAN PLATEAU
HIMALAYAS

Bay of Bengal

BURMA
Rangoon
SIAM
Bangkok
TONKIN
Hanoi
CAMBODIA
COCHIN CHINA
FRENCH INDO-CHINA
Saigon
Hue
ANNAM
Macao (Port.)
Hong Kong (Br.)
Guangzhou
Guangzhou
Fuzhou
TAIWAN (FORMOSA)
OKINAWA

Beijing
Mukden
Port Arthur
Weihaiwei
Qingdao
Nanjing
Shanghai
Hangzhou
Pyongyang
KOREA
Seoul
Pusan

JAPAN
Nagasaki
Osaka
Kyoto
Tokyo

South China Sea

MALAYA
Singapore
SUMATRA
Palembang
Batavia
JAVA
BORNEO
SARAWAK
BRUNEI
BRITISH NORTH BORNEO
DUTCH EAST INDIES
CELEBES
Makassar
PHILIPPINES
Manila
EAST TIMOR (Port.)
Darwin

GERMAN PACIFIC ISLANDS

NEW GUINEA
PAPUA NEW GUINEA

Pacific Ocean

AUSTRALIA
WESTERN AUSTRALIA
NORTHERN TERRITORY
SOUTH AUSTRALIA
QUEENSLAND
NEW SOUTH WALES
VICTORIA
Perth
Melbourne
Sydney
TASMANIA

NEW ZEALAND

©1995 MAGELLAN Geographix℠ Santa Barbara, CA

THE DECLINE OF THE OTTOMAN EMPIRE

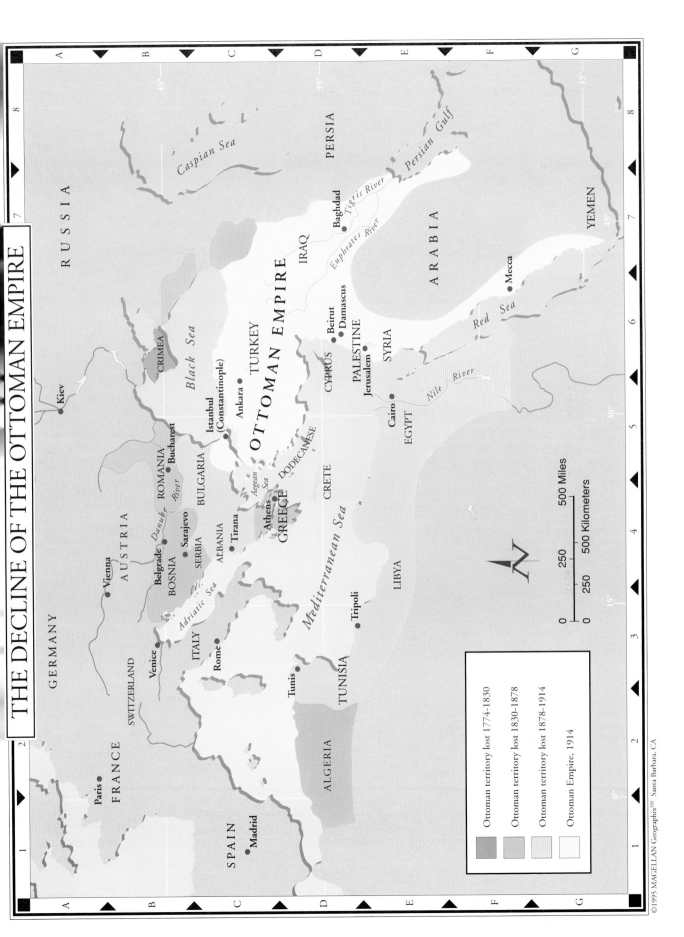

Legend:
- Ottoman territory lost 1774-1830
- Ottoman territory lost 1830-1878
- Ottoman territory lost 1878-1914
- Ottoman Empire, 1914

500 Miles
0   250   500 Kilometers
0   250   500 Kilometers

©1995 MAGELLAN Geographix℠ Santa Barbara, CA

AFRICA, 1914

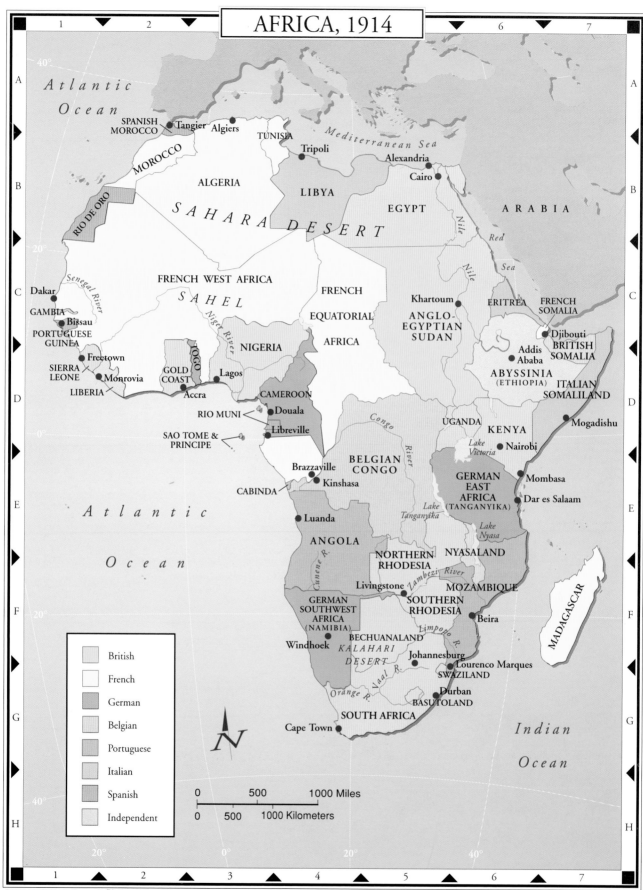

Atlantic Ocean

SPANISH MOROCCO
●Tangier ●Algiers
MOROCCO
TUNISIA
●Tripoli
Mediterranean Sea
●Alexandria
●Cairo
EGYPT
ARABIA

RIO DE ORO

SAHARA DESERT
ALGERIA
LIBYA

20°

Nile
Red Sea

Senegal River
●Dakar
GAMBIA
●Bissau
PORTUGUESE GUINEA
FRENCH WEST AFRICA
SAHEL
Niger River

●Khartoum
ANGLO-EGYPTIAN SUDAN
ERITREA
FRENCH SOMALIA
●Djibouti
BRITISH SOMALIA

FRENCH EQUATORIAL AFRICA

NIGERIA
TOGO
●Freetown
SIERRA LEONE
●Monrovia
LIBERIA
GOLD COAST
●Lagos
●Accra
CAMEROON
RIO MUNI
●Douala
●Libreville
SAO TOME & PRINCIPE

●Addis Ababa
ABYSSINIA (ETHIOPIA)
ITALIAN SOMALILAND
●Mogadishu

0°

UGANDA
KENYA
Congo River
Lake Victoria
●Nairobi

BELGIAN CONGO
●Brazzaville
●Kinshasa
CABINDA

GERMAN EAST AFRICA (TANGANYIKA)
●Mombasa
●Dar es Salaam
Lake Tanganyika

●Luanda
ANGOLA

Lake Nyasa

NORTHERN RHODESIA
NYASALAND
●Livingstone
Zambezi River
MOZAMBIQUE

GERMAN SOUTHWEST AFRICA (NAMIBIA)
SOUTHERN RHODESIA
●Beira

Cunene R.

20°

●Windhoek
BECHUANALAND
KALAHARI DESERT
Limpopo R.
●Johannesburg
●Lourenco Marques
SWAZILAND

Naal R.
Orange R.
●Durban
BASUTOLAND
SOUTH AFRICA
●Cape Town

MADAGASCAR

Atlantic Ocean

Indian Ocean

N

Legend
- British
- French
- German
- Belgian
- Portuguese
- Italian
- Spanish
- Independent

0   500   1000 Miles
0   500   1000 Kilometers

40° 20° 0° 20° 40°

EUROPE, 1914

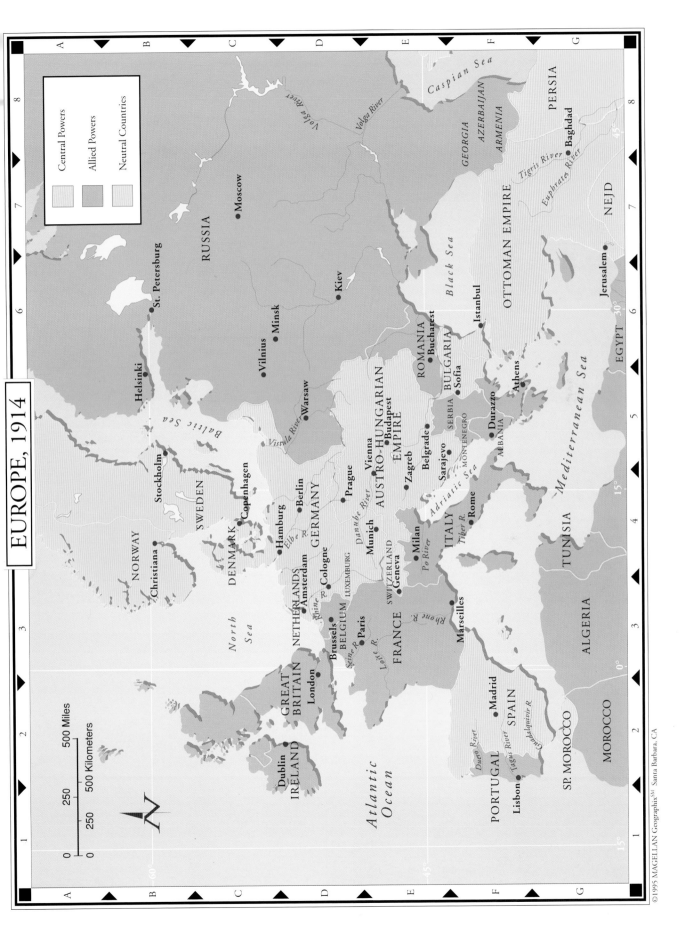

Central Powers
Allied Powers
Neutral Countries

NORWAY
Christiana

SWEDEN
Stockholm

DENMARK
Copenhagen

Helsinki

St. Petersburg

RUSSIA

Moscow

Kiev

Vilnius
Minsk

Warsaw

Baltic Sea

North Sea

GREAT BRITAIN
London

IRELAND
Dublin

NETHERLANDS
Amsterdam

BELGIUM
Brussels

Hamburg
Berlin

GERMANY
Cologne

LUXEMBURG

Prague

Munich

SWITZERLAND
Geneva

AUSTRO-HUNGARIAN EMPIRE
Vienna
Budapest

Zagreb
Belgrade
SERBIA
Sarajevo
MONTENEGRO
ALBANIA
Durazzo

ROMANIA
Bucharest

BULGARIA
Sofia

Athens

Black Sea

OTTOMAN EMPIRE

Istanbul

GEORGIA
AZERBAIJAN
ARMENIA

Caspian Sea

PERSIA

NEJD

Baghdad

Jerusalem

Tigris River
Euphrates River

FRANCE
Paris

Milan
ITALY
Rome

Marseilles

Mediterranean Sea

Adriatic Sea

Tiber R.
Po River

Rhone R.

Seine R.
Loire R.

Rhine R.

Elbe R.
Danube River
Vistula River
Volga River

SPAIN
Madrid

PORTUGAL
Lisbon

Duero River
Tagus River
Guadalquivir R.

SP. MOROCCO
MOROCCO

ALGERIA

TUNISIA

EGYPT

Atlantic Ocean

N

500 Miles
500 Kilometers
0   250   500
0   250   500

60°
45°
15°
0°
15°
30°
45°

©1995 MAGELLAN Geographix℠ Santa Barbara, CA

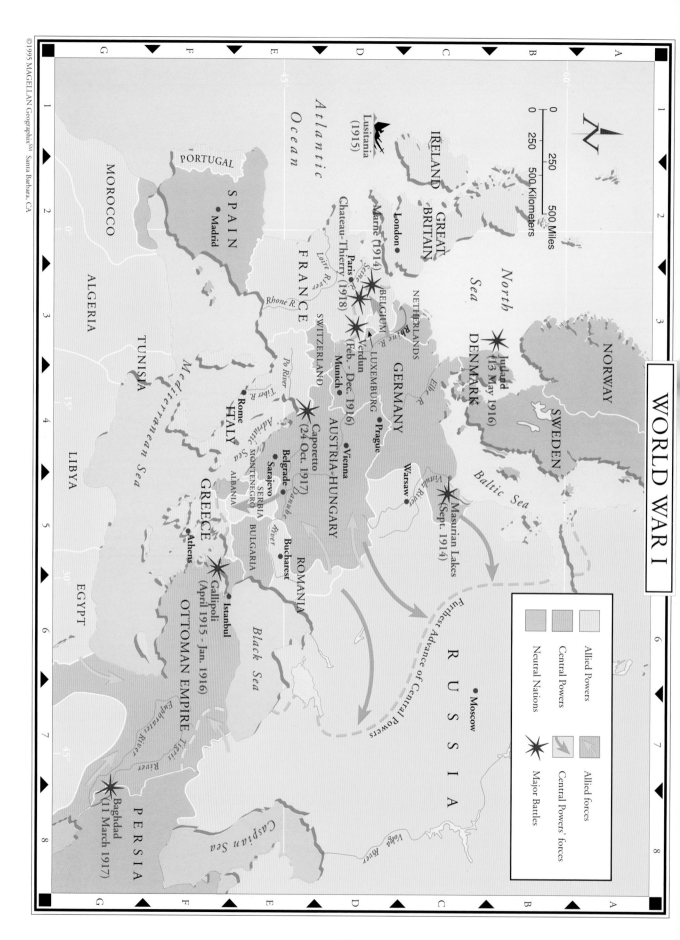

WORLD WAR I

Legend

- Allied Powers
- Central Powers
- Neutral Nations

- Allied forces
- Central Powers' forces
- Major Battles

Battles and events

- Lusitania (1915)
- Jutland (13 May 1916)
- Masurian Lakes (Sept. 1914)
- Marne (1914)
- Chateau-Thierry (1918)
- Verdun (Feb. – Dec. 1916)
- Caporetto (24 Oct. 1917)
- Gallipoli (April 1915 - Jan. 1916)
- Baghdad (11 March 1917)

Places

- Atlantic Ocean
- IRELAND
- GREAT BRITAIN
- London
- PORTUGAL
- SPAIN
- Madrid
- MOROCCO
- ALGERIA
- TUNISIA
- LIBYA
- EGYPT
- Mediterranean Sea
- FRANCE
- Paris
- Seine R.
- Loire River
- Rhone R.
- SWITZERLAND
- BELGIUM
- LUXEMBURG
- NETHERLANDS
- Rhine R.
- GERMANY
- Munich
- Prague
- AUSTRIA-HUNGARY
- Vienna
- Warsaw
- Vistula River
- Elbe R.
- North Sea
- DENMARK
- NORWAY
- SWEDEN
- Baltic Sea
- RUSSIA
- Moscow
- Volga River
- Po River
- ITALY
- Rome
- Tiber R.
- Adriatic Sea
- ALBANIA
- MONTENEGRO
- SERBIA
- Sarajevo
- Belgrade
- Danube River
- BULGARIA
- ROMANIA
- Bucharest
- GREECE
- Athens
- Black Sea
- Istanbul
- OTTOMAN EMPIRE
- Euphrates River
- Tigris River
- PERSIA
- Caspian Sea
- Furthest Advance of Central Powers

©1995 MAGELLAN Geographix℠ Santa Barbara, CA

MIDDLE EAST AFTER WORLD WAR I

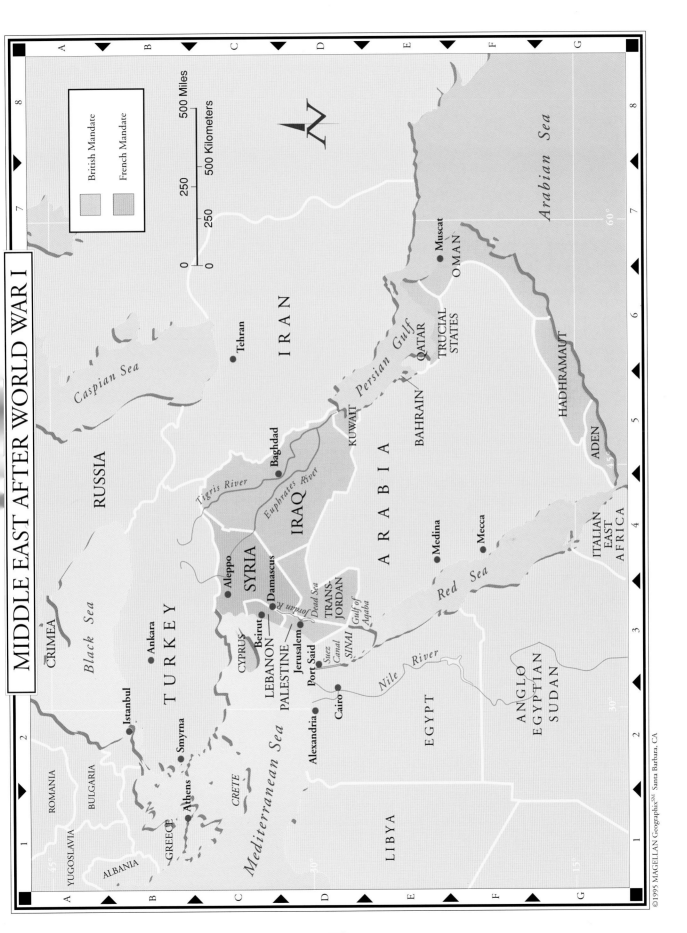

Legend:
British Mandate
French Mandate

500 Miles
500 Kilometers
250
250
0

N

Labels on map:

YUGOSLAVIA
ROMANIA
BULGARIA
ALBANIA
GREECE
Athens
CRETE
Smyrna
Istanbul
TURKEY
Ankara
CRIMEA
Black Sea
RUSSIA
Caspian Sea
Tehran
IRAN
Mediterranean Sea
CYPRUS
Beirut
LEBANON
PALESTINE
Jerusalem
Port Said
Suez Canal
SINAI
Cairo
Alexandria
Nile River
EGYPT
LIBYA
ANGLO EGYPTIAN SUDAN
ITALIAN EAST AFRICA
Aleppo
SYRIA
Damascus
Jordan R.
TRANS-JORDAN
Dead Sea
Gulf of Aqaba
Tigris River
Euphrates River
Baghdad
IRAQ
KUWAIT
ARABIA
Medina
Mecca
Red Sea
Persian Gulf
BAHRAIN
QATAR
TRUCIAL STATES
Muscat
OMAN
Arabian Sea
HADHRAMAUT
ADEN

45°
30°
15°
30°
15°
60°

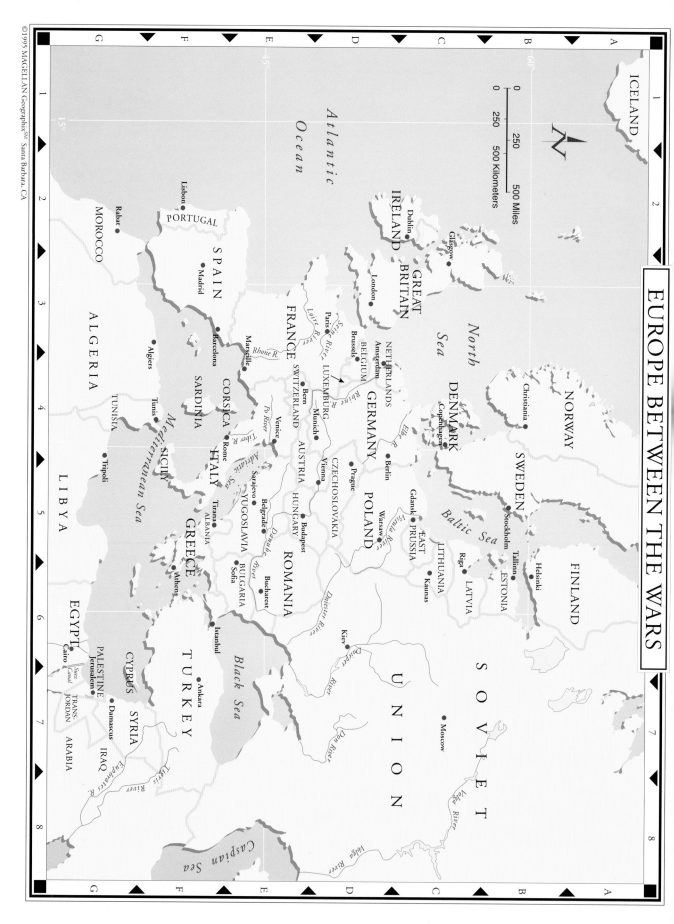

EUROPE BETWEEN THE WARS

©1995 MAGELLAN Geographix℠ Santa Barbara, CA

ICELAND

N

0
250
250
500 Kilometers
500 Miles

Atlantic Ocean

PORTUGAL
Lisbon
MOROCCO
Rabat
SPAIN
Madrid
Barcelona
Algiers
ALGERIA
TUNISIA
Tunis
SARDINIA
CORSICA
Marseille
Rhone R.
FRANCE
Seine River
Loire River
Paris
Brussels
BELGIUM
LUXEMBURG
SWITZERLAND
Bern
Rhine River
NETHERLANDS
Amsterdam
London
GREAT BRITAIN
IRELAND
Dublin
Glasgow
North Sea
DENMARK
Copenhagen
Christiania
NORWAY
SWEDEN
Stockholm
Baltic Sea
Gdansk
EAST PRUSSIA
LITHUANIA
Kaunas
Riga
LATVIA
ESTONIA
Tallinn
Helsinki
FINLAND
GERMANY
Berlin
Munich
CZECHOSLOVAKIA
Prague
Vienna
AUSTRIA
POLAND
Warsaw
Vistula River
Venice
Po River
Tiber R.
Rome
ITALY
SICILY
Adriatic Sea
Mediterranean Sea
Tripoli
LIBYA
Tirana
ALBANIA
GREECE
Athens
YUGOSLAVIA
Sarajevo
Belgrade
HUNGARY
Budapest
ROMANIA
Bucharest
Sofia
BULGARIA
Danube River
Dniester River
Dnieper River
SOVIET UNION
Kiev
Don River
Moscow
Volga River
Volga River
Caspian Sea
Black Sea
Istanbul
TURKEY
Ankara
CYPRUS
SYRIA
Damascus
PALESTINE
Jerusalem
TRANS-JORDAN
Suez Canal
Cairo
EGYPT
ARABIA
IRAQ
Euphrates R.
Tigris River

44

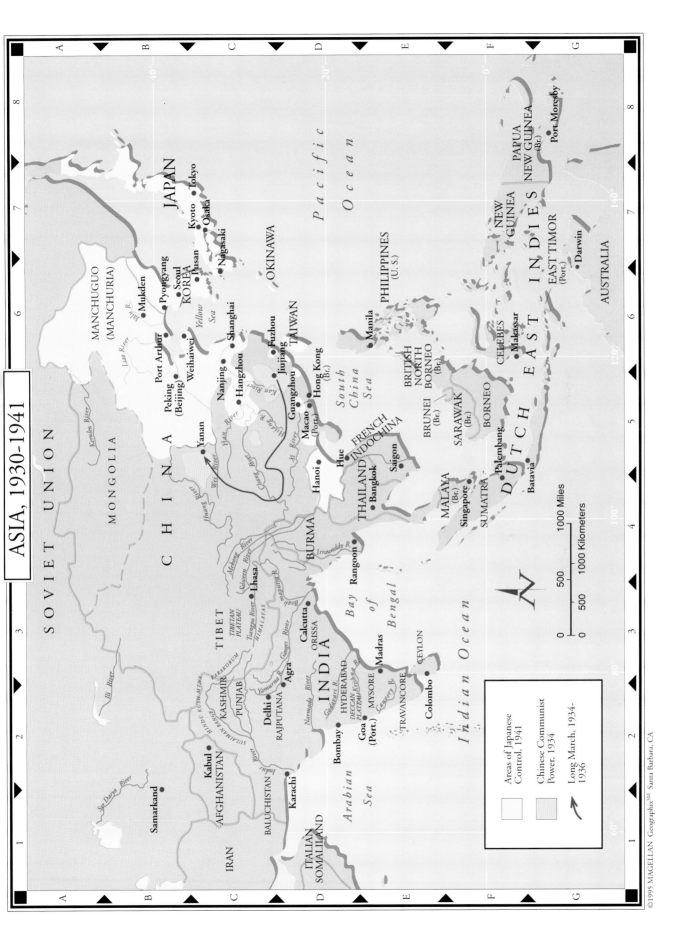

ASIA, 1930-1941

Legend:
- Areas of Japanese Control, 1941
- Chinese Communist Power, 1934
- Long March, 1934-1936

SOVIET UNION

MONGOLIA

MANCHUGUO (MANCHURIA)

CHINA

Kerulen River

Ili River

Syr Darya River

Samarkand

Kabul

AFGHANISTAN

HINDU KUSH MTS.

KARAKORUM

KASHMIR

PUNJAB

SULAIMAN RANGE

BALUCHISTAN

Karachi

RAJPUTANA

Delhi

Agra

Indus River

Yamuna R.

Narmada River

Ganges River

Brahmaputra R.

INDIA

Bombay

Goa (Port.)

HYDERABAD

DECCAN PLATEAU

Krishna R.

Godavari R.

Cauvery R.

MYSORE

Madras

ORISSA

Calcutta

TRAVANCORE

Colombo

CEYLON

Arabian Sea

ITALIAN SOMALILAND

IRAN

Indian Ocean

TIBET

TIBETAN PLATEAU

HIMALAYAS

Lhasa

Tsangpo River

Salween River

Mekong River

Huang River

Wei River

Han River

Chang River

Gan River

Xi River

Yi River

Yanan

Peking (Beijing)

Port Arthur

Weihaiwei

Liao River

Yalu R.

Mukden

Yellow Sea

Nanjing

Hangzhou

Shanghai

Jiujiang

Fuzhou

Guangzhou

Macao (Port.)

Hong Kong (Br.)

TAIWAN

OKINAWA

South China Sea

BURMA

Irrawaddy R.

Rangoon

Bay of Bengal

THAILAND

Bangkok

FRENCH INDOCHINA

Hanoi

Hue

Saigon

MALAYA (Br.)

Singapore

SUMATRA

Palembang

Batavia

DUTCH EAST INDIES

BRITISH NORTH BORNEO (Br.)

BRUNEI (Br.)

SARAWAK (Br.)

BORNEO

CELEBES

Makassar

EAST TIMOR (Port.)

PHILIPPINES (U.S.)

Manila

KOREA

Pyongyang

Seoul

Pusan

JAPAN

Kyoto

Tokyo

Osaka

Nagasaki

Pacific Ocean

NEW GUINEA

PAPUA NEW GUINEA (Br.)

Port Moresby

Darwin

AUSTRALIA

N

Scale:
- 1000 Miles
- 0   500   1000 Kilometers
- 0   500

©1995 MAGELLAN Geographix℠ Santa Barbara, CA

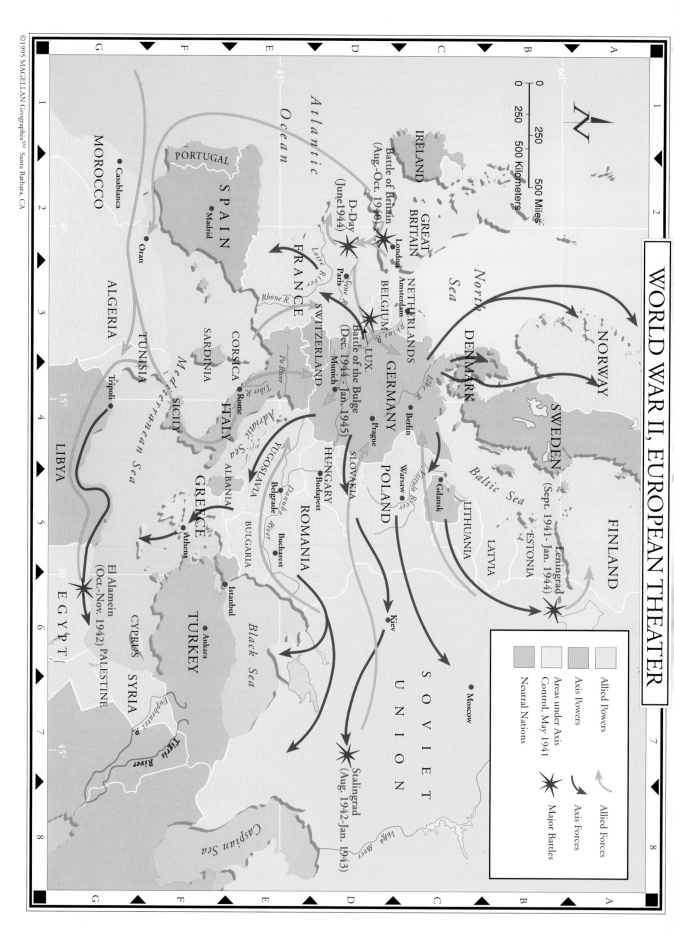

WORLD WAR II, EUROPEAN THEATER

Legend:
- Allied Powers
- Axis Powers
- Areas under Axis Control, May 1941
- Neutral Nations
- Allied Forces
- Axis Forces
- Major Battles

Battle of Britain (Aug.–Oct. 1940)

D-Day (June 1944)

Battle of the Bulge (Dec. 1944–Jan. 1945)

Leningrad (Sept. 1941–Jan. 1944)

Stalingrad (Aug. 1942–Jan. 1943)

El Alamein (Oct.–Nov. 1942)

GREAT BRITAIN, IRELAND, NORWAY, SWEDEN, FINLAND, DENMARK, NETHERLANDS, BELGIUM, LUX., GERMANY, POLAND, SLOVAKIA, HUNGARY, ROMANIA, BULGARIA, YUGOSLAVIA, ALBANIA, GREECE, SWITZERLAND, FRANCE, SPAIN, PORTUGAL, ITALY, SARDINIA, CORSICA, SICILY, ESTONIA, LATVIA, LITHUANIA, SOVIET UNION, TURKEY, CYPRUS, SYRIA, PALESTINE, EGYPT, LIBYA, TUNISIA, ALGERIA, MOROCCO

Cities: London, Amsterdam, Paris, Munich, Berlin, Prague, Warsaw, Gdansk, Budapest, Belgrade, Bucharest, Kiev, Moscow, Rome, Madrid, Casablanca, Oran, Tripoli, Athens, Istanbul, Ankara, Leningrad

Seas/Oceans: Atlantic Ocean, North Sea, Baltic Sea, Mediterranean Sea, Adriatic Sea, Black Sea, Caspian Sea

Rivers: Loire R., Seine R., Rhone R., Rhine R., Elbe R., Po River, Tiber R., Vistula River, Danube River, Volga River, Euphrates R., Tigris River

Scale: 0 250 500 Miles / 0 250 500 Kilometers

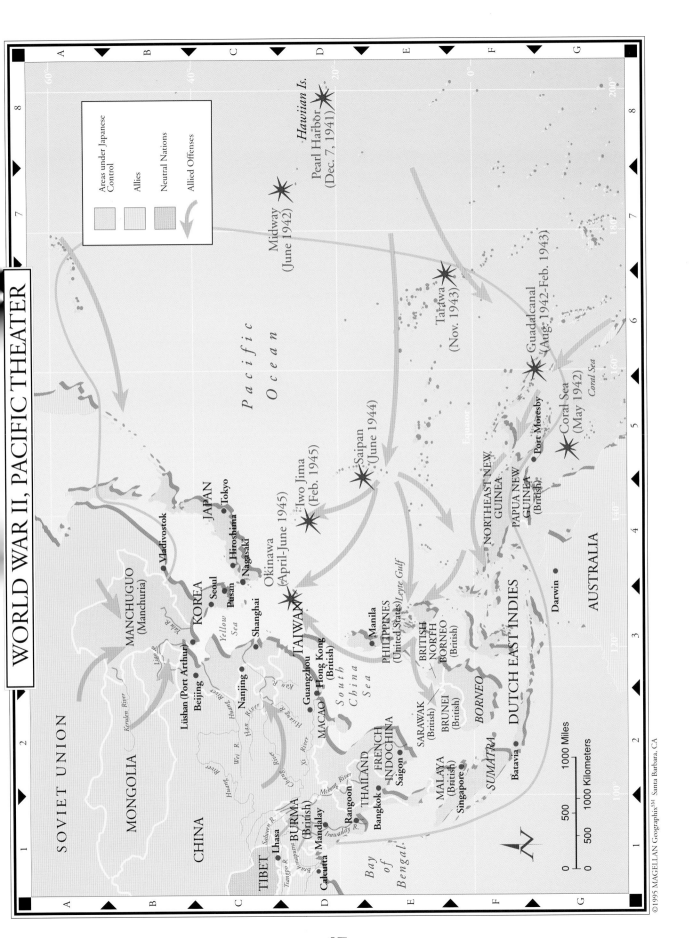

WORLD WAR II, PACIFIC THEATER

Legend:
- Areas under Japanese Control
- Allies
- Neutral Nations
- Allied Offenses

SOVIET UNION

MONGOLIA

CHINA

MANCHUGUO (Manchuria)

TIBET
Lhasa

BURMA (British)
Mandalay
Rangoon

THAILAND
Bangkok

FRENCH INDOCHINA
Saigon

MALAYA (British)
Singapore

SUMATRA
Batavia

Calcutta

Lüshan (Port Arthur)
Beijing
Nanjing
Shanghai

KOREA
Seoul
Pusan

Vladivostok

JAPAN
Tokyo
Hiroshima
Nagasaki

Okinawa (April–June 1945)

TAIWAN

MACAO
Guangzhou
Hong Kong (British)

South China Sea

Yellow Sea

Manila
PHILIPPINES (United States)
Leyte Gulf

BRITISH NORTH BORNEO (British)

SARAWAK (British)
BRUNEI (British)
BORNEO

DUTCH EAST INDIES

Darwin

AUSTRALIA

NORTHEAST NEW GUINEA

PAPUA NEW GUINEA (British)

Port Moresby

Coral Sea (May 1942)

Coral Sea

Guadalcanal (Aug. 1942–Feb. 1943)

Tarawa (Nov. 1943)

Saipan (June 1944)

Iwo Jima (Feb. 1945)

Midway (June 1942)

Pearl Harbor (Dec. 7, 1941)
Hawiian Is.

Pacific Ocean

Equator

Bay of Bengal

Rivers: Kerulen River, Tarim R., Huang River, Wei R., Xi River, Han River, Hsiang R., Kan R., Yangtze, Mekong River, Salween R., Irrawaddy R., Brahmaputra R., Tsangpo R., Yalu R.

1000 Miles
1000 Kilometers
0 500 1000
0 500 1000

N

©1995 MAGELLAN Geographic℠ Santa Barbara, CA

47

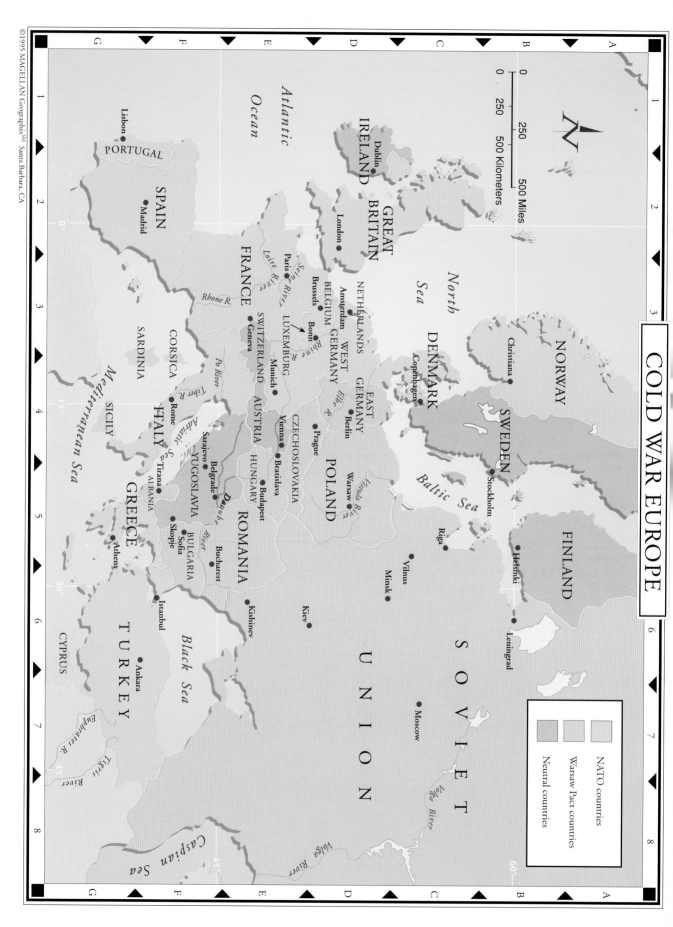

COLD WAR EUROPE

NATO countries

Warsaw Pact countries

Neutral countries

N

0
250   250
500 Kilometers   500 Miles

Atlantic Ocean

Mediterranean Sea

PORTUGAL   Lisbon

SPAIN   Madrid

IRELAND   Dublin

GREAT BRITAIN   London

FRANCE   Paris

Rhone R.   Loire River   Seine River

Brussels   BELGIUM   Amsterdam   NETHERLANDS

LUXEMBURG   Bonn   WEST GERMANY   Rhine R.

SWITZERLAND   Geneva   Munich

AUSTRIA   Vienna   Elbe R.

CORSICA   Po River   ITALY   Rome   Tiber R.

SARDINIA   Adriatic Sea

SICILY

ALBANIA   Tirana

GREECE   Athens

YUGOSLAVIA   Sarajevo   Belgrade

Danube River

HUNGARY   Budapest   Bratislava

CZECHOSLOVAKIA   Prague

EAST GERMANY   Berlin

DENMARK   Copenhagen

NORTH Sea

NORWAY   Christiana

SWEDEN   Stockholm

Baltic Sea

FINLAND   Helsinki

Riga

Vilnus

Minsk

Leningrad

POLAND   Warsaw   Vistula River

ROMANIA   Bucharest

BULGARIA   Sofia   Skopje

Kishinev

Kiev

Istanbul

Black Sea

TURKEY   Ankara

CYPRUS

Euphrates R.   Tigris River

SOVIET UNION   Moscow

Volga River

Caspian Sea

15°   0°   15°   30°   45°   60°

©1995 MAGELLAN Geographix℠ Santa Barbara, CA

THE KOREAN WAR

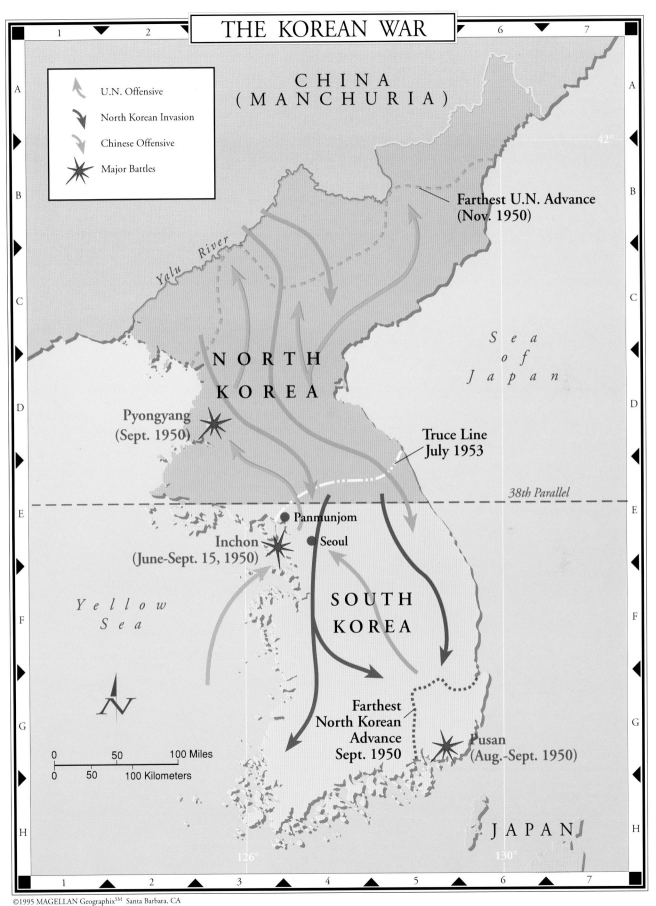

Legend:
- U.N. Offensive
- North Korean Invasion
- Chinese Offensive
- ✳ Major Battles

CHINA (MANCHURIA)

Farthest U.N. Advance (Nov. 1950)

Yalu River

42°

S e a o f J a p a n

N O R T H K O R E A

Pyongyang (Sept. 1950)

Truce Line July 1953

38th Parallel

Panmunjom

Inchon (June-Sept. 15, 1950)

Seoul

Y e l l o w S e a

S O U T H K O R E A

Farthest North Korean Advance Sept. 1950

Pusan (Aug.-Sept. 1950)

N

0   50   100 Miles
0   50   100 Kilometers

126°

130°

J A P A N

©1995 MAGELLAN Geographix℠ Santa Barbara, CA

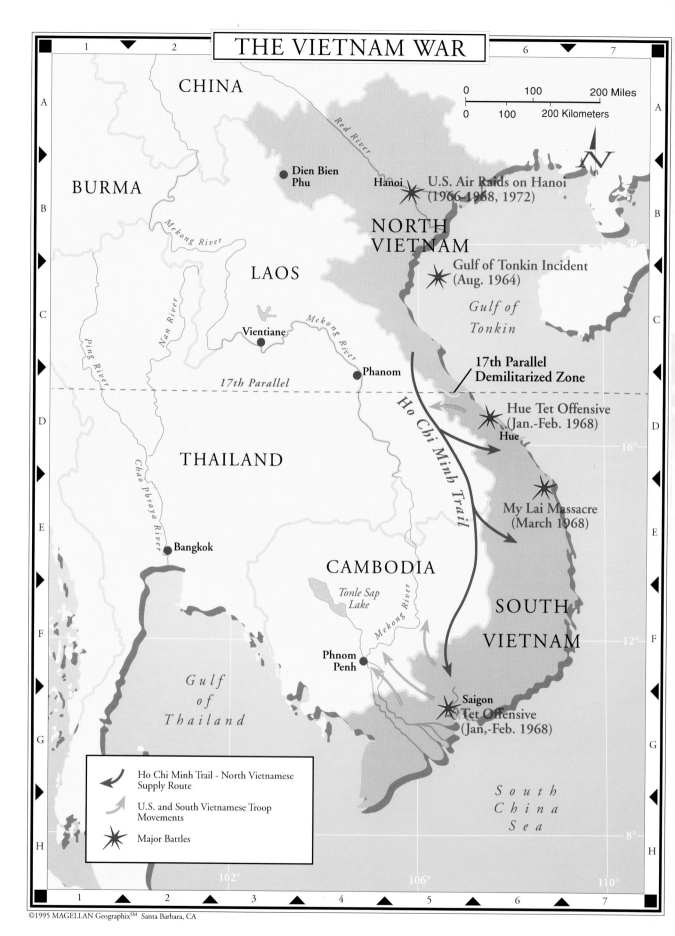

THE VIETNAM WAR

CHINA

Red River

BURMA

Dien Bien Phu

Hanoi

U.S. Air Raids on Hanoi (1966-1968, 1972)

NORTH VIETNAM

Mekong River

LAOS

Gulf of Tonkin Incident (Aug. 1964)

Gulf of Tonkin

Nan River

Vientiane

Mekong River

Phanom

17th Parallel

Ping River

17th Parallel Demilitarized Zone

Ho Chi Minh Trail

Hue Tet Offensive (Jan.-Feb. 1968)

Hue

THAILAND

My Lai Massacre (March 1968)

Chao Phraya River

Bangkok

CAMBODIA

Tonle Sap Lake

SOUTH VIETNAM

Mekong River

Gulf of Thailand

Phnom Penh

Saigon
Tet Offensive (Jan.-Feb. 1968)

South China Sea

Legend:

Ho Chi Minh Trail - North Vietnamese Supply Route

U.S. and South Vietnamese Troop Movements

Major Battles

©1995 MAGELLAN Geographix℠ Santa Barbara, CA

COLD WAR ALLIANCES

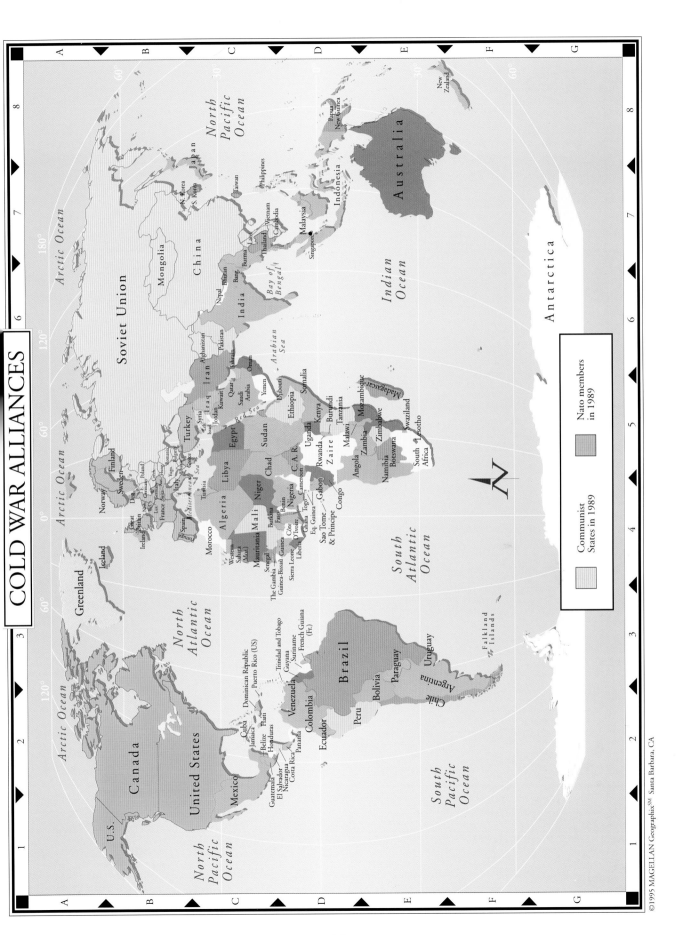

Legend:

Communist States in 1989

Nato members in 1989

©1995 MAGELLAN Geographix℠ Santa Barbara, CA

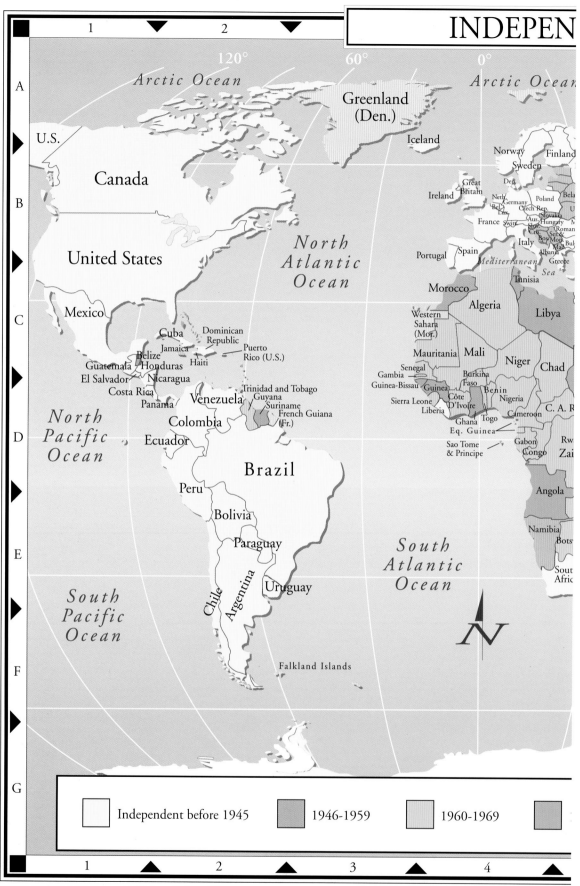

120° 60° 0°

A

Arctic Ocean *Arctic Ocean*

Greenland
(Den.)

Iceland

U.S.

Canada

Norway Finland
Sweden

Great
Britain Den. Poland Bela
Ireland Neth. Germany U.
Bel. Lux. Czech Rep. Slovakia
France Swit. Aus. Hungary Roman
Slov. Cro. Bos. Mon.
Italy Mac. Bul.
Albania Greece

B

United States

Portugal Spain *Mediterranean* *Sea*

Morocco Tunisia

Mexico

Algeria Libya

C

Western
Sahara
(Mor.)

Mauritania Mali Niger Chad

Cuba Dominican
Republic
Jamaica Puerto
Rico (U.S.)
Belize Haiti
Guatemala Honduras
El Salvador Nicaragua
Costa Rica
Panama

Gambia Senegal Burkina
Guinea-Bissau Faso Benin
Guinea Côte Nigeria
Sierra Leone D'Ivoire
Liberia Togo C. A. R
Ghana Cameroon
Eq. Guinea

Trinidad and Tobago
Guyana
Venezuela Suriname
French Guiana
(Fr.)

Colombia

Sao Tome
& Principe Gabon Rw.
Congo Zai

D

*North
Pacific
Ocean*

Ecuador

Brazil

Peru

Angola

Bolivia

Namibia Bots

Paraguay

E

*South
Atlantic
Ocean*

Chile Argentina Uruguay

South
Afric

*South
Pacific
Ocean*

N

F

Falkland Islands

G

*North
Atlantic
Ocean*

☐ Independent before 1945	▨ 1946-1959	▨ 1960-1969	▨

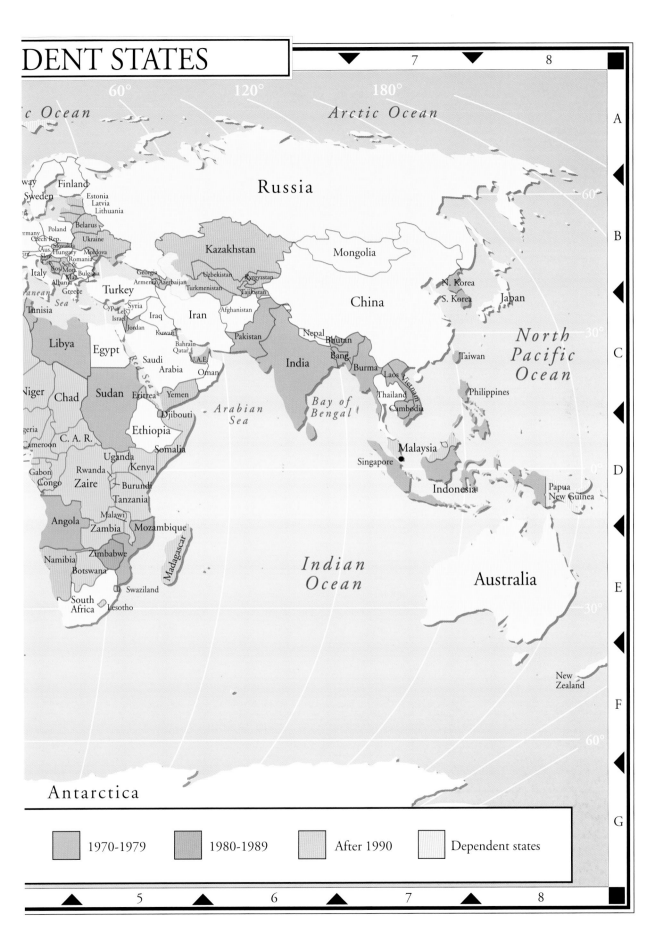

A

B

C

D

E

F

G

60°   **120°**   **180°**

Arctic Ocean

Russia

Finland
Sweden
Estonia
Latvia
Lithuania
Germany Poland
Czech Rep. Belarus
Slovakia Ukraine
Aus. Hungary Moldova
Slo. Ser.& Romania
Italy Bos.Mon. Bulgaria
Albania Greece
Turkey
Tunisia
Mediterranean Sea
Cyp. Leb. Syria Iraq
Israel Jordan
Iran
Kuwait
Libya
Egypt
Saudi Arabia
Bahrain Qatar
U.A.E.
Oman

Georgia
Armenia Azerbaijan
Turkmenistan
Kazakhstan
Uzbekistan
Kyrgyzstan
Tajikistan
Afghanistan
Pakistan

Mongolia

China

N. Korea
S. Korea
Japan

Taiwan

North Pacific Ocean

Nepal
Bhutan
Bang.
India
Burma
Laos
Vietnam
Thailand
Cambodia

Niger
Chad
Sudan
Eritrea
Yemen
Djibouti
Ethiopia
Somalia
C. A. R.
Cameroon
Gabon
Congo
Uganda
Rwanda
Kenya
Zaire
Burundi
Tanzania
Angola
Malawi
Zambia
Mozambique
Zimbabwe
Namibia
Botswana
Madagascar
Swaziland
South Africa
Lesotho

Arabian Sea

Bay of Bengal

Philippines

Malaysia
Singapore

Indonesia

Papua New Guinea

Indian Ocean

Australia

New Zealand

30°

0°

30°

60°

60°

Antarctica

	1970-1979		1980-1989		After 1990		Dependent states

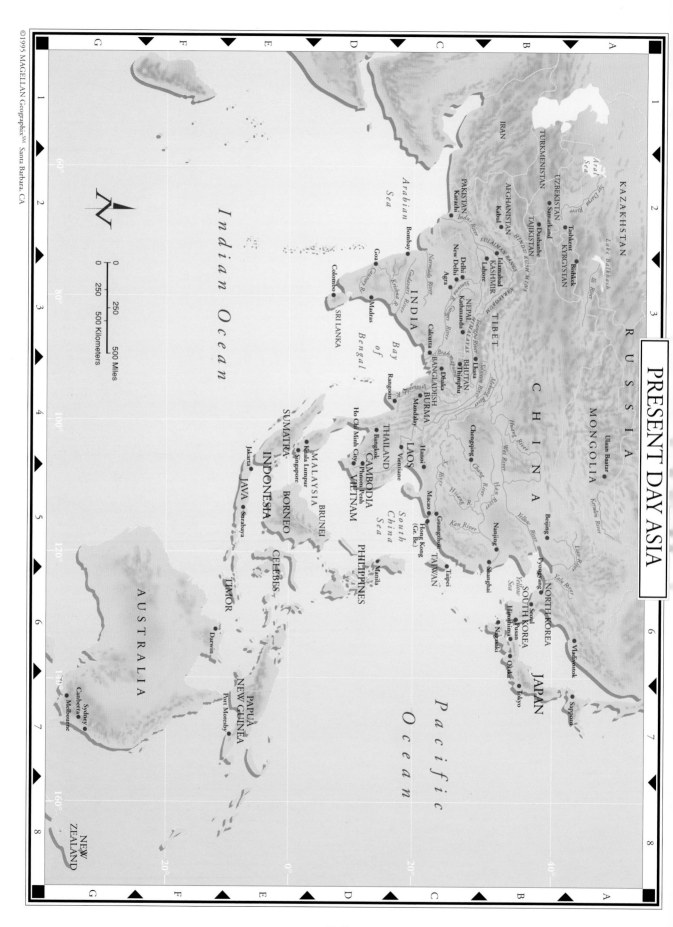

PRESENT DAY ASIA

UNITED STATES

Atlantic Ocean

MEXICO

Houston
New Orleans

Rio Grande R.
Mississippi R.

Gulf of Mexico

Monterrey

BAHAMAS

Miami

Grande de Santiago R.

Guadalajara

Mérida

Havana

CUBA

HAITI

DOMINICAN REPUBLIC
PUERTO RICO

Mexico City
Lake Texcoco
Veracruz

Guantánamo

Port-au-Prince

Santo Domingo

ST. CHRISTOPHER & NEVIS
ANTIGUA & BARBUDA

Acapulco

Oaxaca

Belize City

Kingston

GUATEMALA
BELIZE

JAMAICA

GUADELOUPE

MARTINIQUE

Guatemala

HONDURAS

Caribbean Sea

BARBADOS

EL SALVADOR

San Salvador

Tegucigalpa

NICARAGUA

GRENADA

ST. VINCENT & THE GRENADINES

Managua

San José

Caracas

Lake Maracaibo

Port of Spain

TRINIDAD & TOBAGO

COSTA RICA

Panama City

Panama Canal

PANAMA

VENEZUELA

Bogota

Magdalena R.

Georgetown

Paramaribo

Cayenne

COLOMBIA

FRENCH GUIANA

GUYANA

SURINAME

GALAPAGOS
ISLANDS

Quito

ECUADOR

Amazon R.

Manaus

PERU

Lima

Ucayali R.
Urubamba R.

Recife

BRAZIL

Paraguay River

BOLIVIA

Lake Titicaca

La Paz

Brasilia

Pacific Ocean

CHILE

PARAGUAY

São Paulo

Rio de Janeiro

Asunción

Paraná River

Valparaiso
Santiago

Rosario

URUGUAY
Montevideo

Buenos Aires

ARGENTINA

FALKLAND
ISLANDS

CAPE HORN

N

PRESENT DAY AFRICA

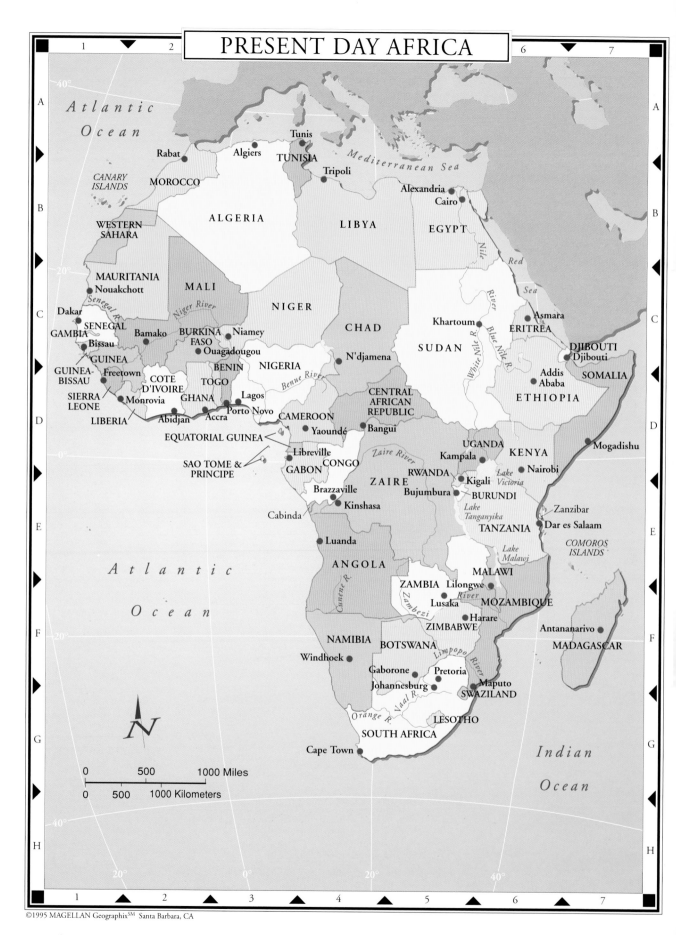

Atlantic Ocean

CANARY ISLANDS

Mediterranean Sea

Rabat
Algiers
Tunis
TUNISIA
Tripoli
Alexandria
Cairo

MOROCCO
ALGERIA
LIBYA
EGYPT

Nile
Red Sea

WESTERN SAHARA

MAURITANIA
Nouakchott
MALI
Senegal R.
Niger River
NIGER
CHAD
Khartoum
Asmara
ERITREA

Dakar
SENEGAL
GAMBIA
Bissau
GUINEA-BISSAU
GUINEA
Bamako
BURKINA FASO
Ouagadougou
Niamey
SUDAN
DJIBOUTI
Djibouti
White Nile R.
Blue Nile R.

Freetown
SIERRA LEONE
Monrovia
LIBERIA
COTE D'IVOIRE
Abidjan
BENIN
TOGO
GHANA
Accra
Porto Novo
NIGERIA
N'djamena
Benue River
Addis Ababa
SOMALIA
ETHIOPIA

Lagos
CENTRAL AFRICAN REPUBLIC

EQUATORIAL GUINEA
SAO TOME & PRINCIPE
CAMEROON
Yaoundé
Bangui
UGANDA
Kampala
KENYA
Mogadishu

Libreville
CONGO
GABON
Zaire River
RWANDA
Kigali
Nairobi
Lake Victoria

Brazzaville
Kinshasa
ZAIRE
Bujumbura
BURUNDI
Lake Tanganyika
Zanzibar
Dar es Salaam

Cabinda
TANZANIA
COMOROS ISLANDS

Luanda
Lake Malawi

ANGOLA
MALAWI
Lilongwe
MOZAMBIQUE

ZAMBIA
Lusaka
Zambezi River
Harare
Antananarivo
MADAGASCAR

Cunene R.
ZIMBABWE

NAMIBIA
BOTSWANA
Limpopo River

Windhoek
Gaborone
Pretoria
Maputo
SWAZILAND

Johannesburg
Vaal R.
LESOTHO

Orange R.
SOUTH AFRICA
Cape Town

Atlantic Ocean

Indian Ocean

N

0   500   1000 Miles
0   500   1000 Kilometers

40° 20° 0° 20° 40°

PRESENT DAY MIDDLE EAST

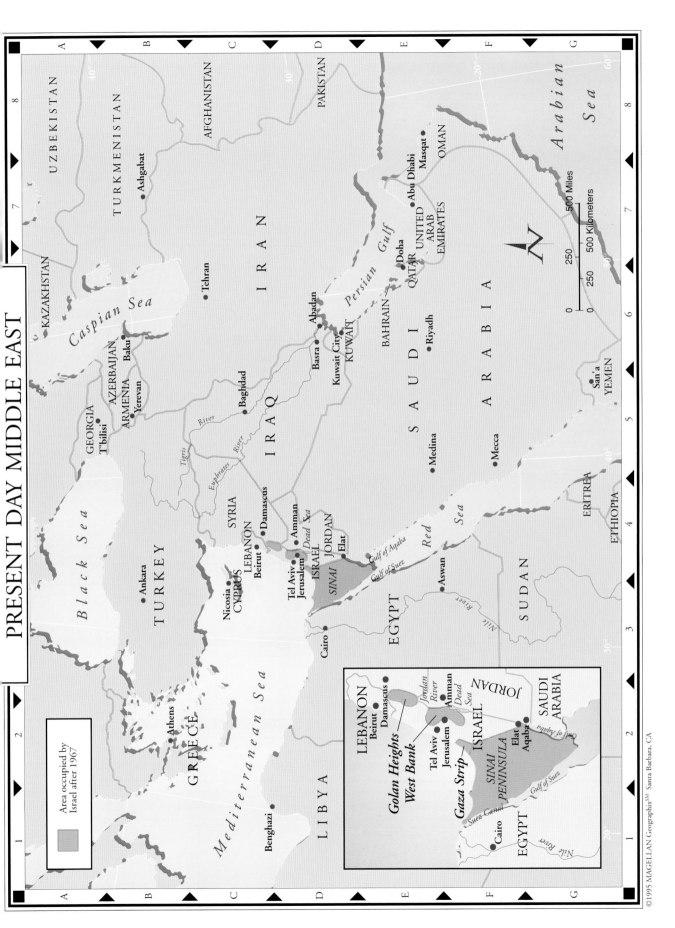

Area occupied by
Israel after 1967

© 1995 MAGELLAN Geographix℠ Santa Barbara, CA

57

PRESENT DAY EUROPE

ICELAND

FAROE ISLANDS (Den.)

Atlantic Ocean

IRELAND
Dublin

GREAT BRITAIN
London

PORTUGAL
Lisbon

Tagus River
Guadalquivir R.

SPAIN
Madrid

FRANCE
Paris
Seine River
Loire River
Rhone R.

BELGIUM
Brussels
LUXEMBURG
Bonn
Amsterdam
NETHERLANDS

GERMANY
Berlin
Rhine R.
Elbe River

DENMARK
Copenhagen

North Sea

NORWAY
Oslo

SWEDEN
Stockholm

FINLAND
Helsinki

Baltic Sea

ESTONIA
Tallinn

Sr. Petersburg

RUSSIA

LATVIA
Riga

LITHUANIA
Vilnus

BELARUS
Minsk

Moscow

Vistula River

POLAND
Warsaw

CZECH REPUBLIC
Prague

SWITZERLAND
Geneva

AUSTRIA
Vienna

SLOVENIA
Ljubljana

HUNGARY
Budapest

SLOVAKIA
Bratislava

UKRAINE
Kiev

MOLDOVA
Kishinev

ROMANIA
Bucharest

Danube River

CROATIA
Zagreb

BOSNIA HERZEGOVINA
Sarajevo

YUGOSLAVIA
Belgrade

BULGARIA
Sofia

MACEDONIA
Skopje

ALBANIA
Tirana

GREECE
Athens

ITALY
Rome
Po River
Tiber R.
Adriatic Sea

CORSICA

SARDINIA

SICILY

Mediterranean Sea

TURKEY
Ankara
Istanbul

Black Sea

CYPRUS

Euphrates R.
Tigris River

Volga River

15°
0°
15°
30°
45°

60°

N
0 250 500 Kilometers
0 250 500 Miles

Member nations of the European Community

A B C D E F G
1 2 3 4 5 6 7 8

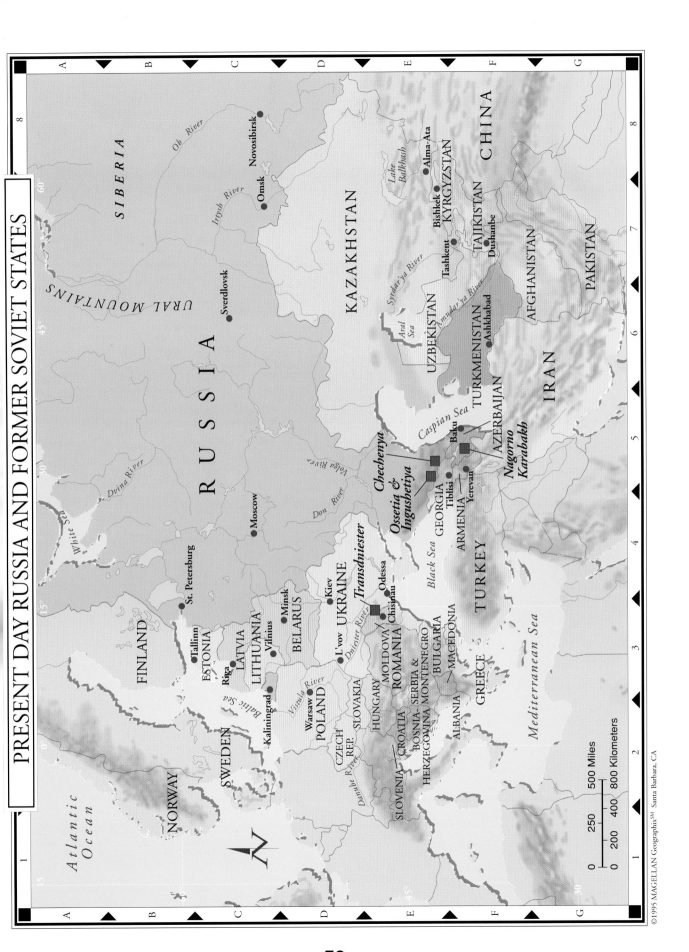

PRESENT DAY RUSSIA AND FORMER SOVIET STATES

Atlantic Ocean

NORWAY
SWEDEN
FINLAND
Tallinn
ESTONIA
Riga
LATVIA
LITHUANIA
Vilnius
Kaliningrad
Warsaw
POLAND
Baltic Sea
Vistula River

St. Petersburg

SIBERIA

URAL MOUNTAINS
Sverdlovsk

R U S S I A
Moscow

Ob River
Irtysh River
Omsk
Novosibirsk

White Sea
Dvina River
Don River
Volga River

Minsk
BELARUS
Kiev
L'vov UKRAINE
Dniester River
Transdniester
Odessa
Chisinau
MOLDOVA
ROMANIA

CZECH REP.
SLOVAKIA
HUNGARY
SLOVENIA
CROATIA
BOSNIA-HERZEGOVINA
SERBIA & MONTENEGRO
MACEDONIA
BULGARIA
ALBANIA
GREECE
Danube River

Black Sea

Chechenya
Ossetia & Ingushetiya

GEORGIA
Tbilisi
ARMENIA
Yerevan
AZERBAIJAN
Baku
Nagorno Karabakh

Caspian Sea

TURKEY

Mediterranean Sea

KAZAKHSTAN

Aral Sea
Lake Balkhash
Alma-Ata
Bishkek
KYRGYZSTAN
Tashkent
TAJIKISTAN
Dushanbe
UZBEKISTAN
Syrdar'ya River
Amudar'ya River
TURKMENISTAN
Ashkhabad

CHINA

AFGHANISTAN
IRAN
PAKISTAN

N

500 Miles
800 Kilometers
0 250 500
0 200 400

©1995 MAGELLAN Geographix℠ Santa Barbara, CA

59

PRESENT DAY WORLD

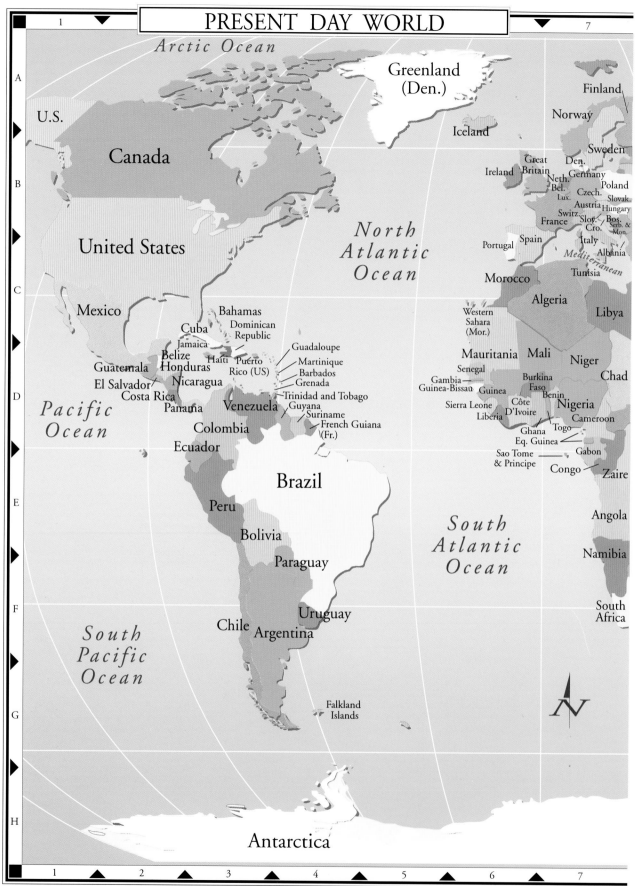

Arctic Ocean

Greenland
(Den.)

Finland

Norway

U.S.

Canada

Iceland

Sweden

Great
Britain
Den.

Ireland
Neth.
Germany
Bel.
Poland
Lux.
Czech.
Slovak.
Austria
Hungary
Switz.
Slov.
France
Cro.
Bos.
Serb. &
Mon.

North
Atlantic
Ocean

Portugal
Spain
Italy
Albania

Mediterranean

United States

Morocco
Tunisia

Western
Sahara
(Mor.)
Algeria
Libya

Mexico

Bahamas

Cuba
Dominican
Republic

Jamaica

Mauritania
Mali
Niger
Chad

Guadaloupe

Belize
Haiti
Puerto
Martinique
Rico (US)

Senegal

Guatemala
Honduras
Barbados
Gambia
Burkina
Faso

El Salvador
Nicaragua
Grenada
Guinea-Bissau
Guinea
Benin
Nigeria

Costa Rica
Trinidad and Tobago

Pacific
Ocean
Panama
Venezuela
Guyana
Sierra Leone
Côte
D'Ivoire
Cameroon

Suriname
Liberia
Ghana
Togo

Colombia
French Guiana
(Fr.)
Eq. Guinea
Gabon

Ecuador
Sao Tome
& Principe
Congo
Zaire

Brazil

Peru

South
Atlantic
Ocean
Angola

Bolivia

Namibia

Paraguay

South
Pacific
Ocean
Uruguay

Chile
Argentina
South
Africa

Falkland
Islands

Antarctica

©1995 MAGELLAN Geographix℠ Santa Barbara, CA

60

Arctic Ocean

A

Finland
Estonia
Latvia
Lithuania

Russia

B

Belarus
Ukraine
Moldova
Romania
Bulgaria
Macedonia
Greece
Sea
Leb.
Israel
Jordan

Georgia
Armenia Azerbaijan
Turkey
Turkmenistan
Syria
Iraq
Iran

Kazakhstan
Uzbekistan

Kyrgyzstan
Tajikistan

Mongolia

N. Korea
S. Korea Japan

China

North
Pacific
Ocean

C

Egypt

Sudan

Kuwait
Qatar
Saudi
Arabia
Oman

Bahrain
U. A. E.

Afghanistan

Pakistan

Nepal

India

Bhutan
Bang.
Myanmar
(Burma)

Taiwan

Macao

Eritrea
Djibouti

Yemen

Red Sea

Arabian
Sea

Laos
Thailand
Vietnam
Cambodia

Philippines

D

C.A.R.

Ethiopia

Somalia

Bay of
Bengal

Sri Lanka

Singapore

Brunei
Malaysia

Borneo

Uganda
Rwanda
Zaire
Burundi
Kenya
Tanzania

Sumatra

Indonesia

Java

Papua
New Guinea

E

Malawi
Zambia
Zimbabwe
Botswana
South
Africa

Mozambique
Madagascar

Swaziland
Lesotho

Indian
Ocean

Australia

F

New
Zealand

G

H

Antarctica

INDEX